Home for Dinner

A Real Estate Novel

Robert Lee

Lesix Companies LLC

Home for Dinner

Being present and happy for my wife, Blair, and my girls, Blake and Dylan, is my greatest calling and my greatest inspiration.

THE BREAKING POINT

Wade Roberts pulled into his driveway at 9:47 PM and did not turn off the engine.

The house was dark except for the kitchen. One light, the pendant over the sink that Peyton left on when she was waiting up and didn't want to look like she was waiting up. He'd learned to read that light the way sailors read weather. Not by what it showed, but by what it meant about what was coming.

He sat there with the car running, the AC pushing stale air against his face, and scrolled back through his phone. The texts from Peyton formed a timeline he already knew by heart because he'd watched them arrive all afternoon and done nothing about any of them.

2:36 PM: Just confirming you'll be home by 5 for Kelli's party?

He'd seen that one while pulling into the Hendersons' driveway for a listing appointment he'd chased for three weeks. The Hendersons, who spent forty-five minutes walking him through their renovations and then told him they were "still interviewing agents." He'd smiled and said he understood. He meant neither of those things.

4:52 PM: The girls are excited! They keep asking when you'll be here.

That one came during an open house on Birch Lane. Only four visitors. Two of them, an overly inquisitive couple, were just neighbors checking on the renovation progress. One was a woman who took a flyer and used the bathroom. The fourth asked if he could come see it again next Tuesday and then never responded to the confirmation text.

6:15 PM: We're going ahead with cake. She keeps asking for you.

He'd been sitting in the parking lot of a Chick-fil-A at that point, working up a listing presentation for a lead he'd gotten off a postcard mailer. He remembered thinking: I'll leave in twenty minutes. Thirty tops. I just need to finish this one thing.

8:03 PM: She cried herself to sleep. Thinks she did something wrong.

Wade turned off the engine.

The front walk was scattered with chalk drawings. This was Kelli's work from earlier in the day, when the party was still ahead of her; when this might have been a world where her father kept his promises. He could see a lopsided birthday cake with five candles. A stick-figure family: Peyton tall, Amelia beside her, Kelli with enormous curly hair, and a smaller figure off to the side with something in its hand. A phone, probably.

The front door was unlocked. It was always unlocked when Peyton was angry. She tended to forget minor things like that, or wanted Wade to know exactly what he was about to walk into. He was never completely sure.

The kitchen smelled like cold pizza and sugar. An ice cream cake, Kelli's favorite, the one with the crunch layer in the middle, sat on the counter, half-eaten and melting into its cardboard base. Purple streamers hung from the light fixture. A stack of paper plates with cartoon unicorns sat mostly unused beside a pile of torn wrapping paper. The party was small. Just them. Kelli had wanted to have fun with mommy, daddy, and sister. She'd been specific about it.

He counted the place settings. Four. Kelli's still had a party hat sitting on the plate, the elastic chin strap curled like a question mark.

Peyton was at the table.

Not eating. Not reading. Not doing anything that would give him a natural opening to say something normal, something that could ease them past this moment. She was just sitting with a glass of water and the particular stillness of a woman who had already decided what she was going to say. She just waited for the other person to arrive so she could say it and go to bed.

The night before, she'd come off a twelve-hour shift at seven in the morning working with one struggling unit. She slept until noon after Wade left her that morning, then spent the afternoon setting up a birthday party for a five-year-old who wanted nothing except her whole family in one room with a cake. Peyton had given her three out of four. Wade could see in the set of her jaw what that fraction had cost her.

"Hey," she said.

"Hey," he meekly replied.

He stood in the doorway like a man entering a room he wasn't sure he was allowed in. "I'm sorry. The Henderson thing went long, and then I had the open house, and I thought I could make it back by"

"Wade."

"—six, maybe six-thirty, and then the listing presentation—"

"Wade."

He stopped.

Peyton looked at him. Not through him. Just at him. The way she looked at patients' families when she was about to tell them something true that they weren't going to want to hear. Not cruel, but steady.

"She asked me four times if you were coming," Peyton said. "Four times. And I told her yes every time because I believed you. Then she asked a fifth time and I couldn't say it anymore, so I told her you were trying, and she said, 'Trying means no.' She didn't talk much the rest of the night."

Wade didn't have a response to that. He opened his mouth and nothing useful was in it.

"She's five, Wade. She's five years old and she already knows that 'trying' is what people say when they're not going to do the thing," Peyton said. As she said it, her mouth started to quiver and her tone showed she was emotionally spent.

"I know."

"Do you?" Peyton's tone immediately changed. Now, her anger was starting to show.

The kitchen stood quiet for that next moment except for the refrigerator humming. The slow drip of the ice cream cake finding its way off the edge of the cardboard onto the counter was even audible. Peyton watched him the way she'd been watching him for months. This was the careful attention of someone measuring the distance between where a person is and where they need to be. She was calculating whether the gap is still crossable.

"I'm not asking you to choose between your career and your family," she said. "You have to figure out how to have both. Because right now, you don't have either."

She let that land. She was good at that; at saying the thing and then not rushing to soften it. She'd learned it in the ICU, or maybe she'd always been that way and the ICU had just given her a place where it was useful. Either way, the silence after her sentences always carried more weight than other people's follow-up statements.

Wade started to say something, but stopped. He wasn't sure what to say. Something about a plan, about changes he'd make, about tomorrow were all just empty. But Peyton was already standing.

"I set Amelia's alarm for six so she could show you the card she made for Kelli before school." She carried her glass to the sink. "So be up."

She walked past him toward the hallway. At the doorway she paused. For a moment he thought she might say something else, something softer, something that would let him breathe. Instead she said, "There's pizza in the fridge," and then he heard her footsteps on the stairs and the quiet click of their bedroom door.

Not a slam. A click. Which was worse, and she knew it was worse.

And he knew she knew.

Wade didn't go upstairs. He sat down at the dining room table, which was the place his family was supposed to eat dinner together. It served more as his makeshift desk. Every piece of his professional life accumulated like sediment.

He cleared a space by pushing more things to the side. Peyton stopped commenting on that habit months ago. For her, it was like complaining about the weather. She hated the clutter, but complaints wouldn't change anything for her.

His tablet was buried under a stack of For Sale flyers he'd printed for the Birch Lane open house. Forty copies. He'd handed out six. The top few on the stack curled at the edges from humidity.

He opened the tablet. He wanted to avoid his laptop that had a browser full of tabs waiting to scream at him. So many tabs that they compressed into a bar of indistinguishable favicons. Not to mention his word processor, email, and a few messenger services he subscribed to were also open so he could float between them all.

He knew what was in there without looking: three articles on Facebook ad targeting he'd bookmarked and never read; a YouTube video titled "5 AI Tools Every Agent Needs in 2024" that he'd watched the first four minutes of; two competing blog posts about whether door-knocking was dead or the secret to a seven-figure business; a Canva template for "Just Sold" postcards he'd started customizing and abandoned; a half-finished Google Form for client testimonials; the login pages for three different CRMs he'd switched between twice in eighteen months and still had active subscriptions for. Combined cost: $547 a month for software he used the way most people use gym memberships.

Also on the table: a shoebox of business cards from networking events. BNI breakfasts he'd attended as a guest, chamber mixers, a mortgage lender's happy hour, and who knows how many real estate events. Each card represented a conversation he'd had and a follow-up he'd intended to make. He'd followed up on maybe a third. The rest had aged past the point where a call would feel natural and into the territory where it would feel like what it was: a man remembering too late that he'd forgotten something important.

He pulled up his transaction spreadsheet. He didn't need to, he knew the numbers. It felt like the balance of a checking account that's always lower than you need it to be. He looked anyway. The feeling in his chest was the same as pressing a bruise. He wanted to press to punish himself if nothing else.

He was wrapping up year three. Gross commission: $67,412. Before the brokerage split, before the E&O insurance, before the MLS and forms dues, before the three CRMs, before the lead generation subscription he'd signed up for in a moment of optimism and couldn't cancel for another four months, before the gas for the twenty-two thousand miles he'd put on his car driving to showings and open houses and listing appointments that went nowhere.

Net take-home after expenses: $41,200. Divided by the roughly three thousand hours he'd worked, and he had worked them, every one, he could account for the time. That came out to $13.73 an hour.

Peyton made more than six figures as an ICU manager. Even still, she worked irregular hours at times because she felt the responsibility of running a tight ship. She'd been doing nights lately to oversee and guide the 7 PM to 7 AM rotation. The staff needed leadership they weren't getting, so she took charge. She slept during the day while the girls were at school and worked while they were sleeping. She wouldn't admit to him that she worked this hard so Wade could keep doing what he was doing.

He closed the spreadsheet, turned off the tablet, and took a deep breath. The past week assembled itself in his mind without being invited. He didn't resist the mental exercise, but he also knew it wouldn't lead to anything meaningful.

Thursday was three hours of cold calls from a purchased lead list. Two people answered. One hung up. One asked to be removed from whatever list this was.

Friday was door-knocking in a subdivision in Kennesaw. Fourteen doors. Four answered. One was interested enough to take a card but not interested enough to give a name.

Saturday brought the Henderson listing appointment. Three weeks of pursuit, forty-five minutes of their time, and a polite rejection dressed as deliberation.

Monday was a buyer showing that seemed to go well until the clients mentioned they'd spoken with the listing agent on their own. They'd seen the home three or four weeks earlier; just wanted to confirm what their gut had already told them: it wasn't a good fit.

Tuesday was the open house on Birch Lane and the Chick-fil-A parking lot and Kelli's birthday party happening without him a few miles away.

Every one of those activities was something the industry told him to do. Cold calls. Door knocking. Open houses. Networking. Lead follow-up. Social media content. He was doing all of it, the full playbook. He did everything he was told by his broker who preached it in Monday meetings with the enthusiasm of a carnival game barker. Wade was playing the numbers game, but it was hard to stay positive.

It all felt like a key for the wrong lock. You can push harder. You can jiggle it. You can curse at it. But the mechanism doesn't engage because the mechanism was never designed for that key, and no amount of effort changes the engineering.

Wade didn't have that metaphor yet. He just knew the numbers, and the numbers were a wall he kept running into. Each collision looked exactly like the last one, but felt worse.

The house settled around him as he doom scrolled his memory of the past week. Small sounds that only exist when nobody's talking. The ice maker cycled. The cake continued its slow collapse on the counter. A small click in the hallway that could have been Peyton quietly checking whether her husband was still awake.

Wade leaned back in the chair and his eyes found the refrigerator. It was covered in the usual archaeology of family life; school lunch menus, a magnet from the pediatric dentist, a crayon drawing of what appeared to be a horse or possibly a large dog. And a photograph, pinned under a Braves magnet, of his father standing next to a 1987 Ford F-150 with the hood up.

Jon Roberts. Fifty-two years in the same town. Forty-one of those years working at the same shop, the last twenty as owner. When old man Cahill retired and sold it to him for a dollar and a handshake, Jon jumped in and never looked back. Six days a week, sometimes seven during deer season when every truck in the county needed something fixed before the opener. A mechanic who came home with grease under his nails that never fully came out. His hands smelled like Gojo and motor oil even on Sundays.

And he never missed a game.

That was the part Wade kept circling back to, the part that didn't add up no matter how many times he tried to make the math work. Jon Roberts worked six days a week in a shop that opened at seven and closed when the last car was done. He had no back office staff, no expensive computer system, or a background as an entrepreneur. He ran everything with a pegboard and a spiral notebook where he wrote down what he'd done and what it cost. He ran that business with his hands, a pencil, a few mechanics who would follow him into any battle, and a memory for faces that bordered on supernatural.

He never missed a single one of Wade's baseball games. Not the Tuesday afternoon JV games where Wade sat on the bench.

Not the Saturday tournaments two towns over. He made a point of telling everyone he was going to watch his son in the state playoff game junior year. A game that started at four o'clock on a Wednesday. He felt so bad about leaving his guys that he offered to close the shop early. They stayed and kept it open without him. Jon's boys wouldn't let the shop lose an afternoon's revenue stream for the privilege of watching his son go 0-for-3 with a walk.

Wade remembered looking up from the on-deck circle and finding him, always in the same spot. The third row behind the home dugout, ball cap pulled low, work shirt still on. He never cheered loudly. He'd clap, steady and even, the way he did most things. And afterward, win or lose, the same question: "Did you have fun out there?"

Never a lecture on what to do better. Never a rhetorical question like why did you swing at that? Just: did you have fun?

Wade had always chalked it up to a different era. Simpler times. A small-town mechanic's life didn't have the same demands as a real estate career in metropolitan Atlanta. Jon didn't have forty-seven browser tabs and three CRMs and a phone that buzzed with other people's urgency sixteen hours a day. He had a shop and a notebook. He lived in a town small enough to drive across in twelve minutes.

That was the story Wade told himself. It was comfortable, and it was almost entirely wrong. But he was sitting at a dining room table covered in evidence of his own failure at 10:30 on a Tuesday night. Fleeting comfort was the only currency he could still afford.

He thought about calling his mother. She'd be awake. She was always awake since Jon died eighteen months ago, as if sleep were a luxury that belonged to a version of her life that no longer existed. But he didn't want to hear the thing she'd say, which was the thing she always said, which was: "Your father would want you to be happy, Wade." Because he didn't know what that meant anymore. He suspected his mother didn't either. He just didn't want to walk into that room.

At some point Wade opened his laptop. He wasn't sure when; the kitchen clock had become one more thing he wasn't looking at. He started closing the old ones without even looking for their value. Not all of them. Thirty, roughly, deleted with the mechanical efficiency of a man cleaning a garage who doesn't want to think about what he's throwing away. He told himself this was simplification and progress. It was just the same thing he did every time the accumulation of abandoned strategies became too visible to ignore. Purging felt like action and changed nothing about the system that produced the mess.

He closed the laptop and set it on top of the sleeping tablet. He kept a stack of blank notecards on the table for the follow-up notes he was always going to write and rarely did. He picked up a pen and wrote a list.

Tomorrow:

— Up by 5:00.

— Gym.

— 50 calls before 10.

— Follow up on Henderson (email, not call. Less pressure)

— Birch Lane price reduction conversation with seller

— New lead gen strategy / research options

— Home by 6. No exceptions.

He underlined *No exceptions* twice. Then he looked at it, added See Amelia's card @ 6, and felt the familiar warmth of a plan. Felt like the pull of a narcotic. His belief that the effort would be the one that worked was warming to his soul. He'd felt it before.

After every bad month, after every hard conversation with Peyton, after every Monday morning sales meeting where his broker's enthusiasm briefly became contagious. The plan always felt true at 11 PM.

Like any drug, the warmth gave way to emptiness. By Thursday it would be buried under the same reactive chaos that had eaten every plan before it. He refused to admit that yet. Or he did and couldn't afford to. It amounted to the same thing.

He stood up and carried the notecard to the refrigerator. Moved the Braves magnet off the photo of his father, pinned the notecard in its place, then put the photo back beside it. Jon and the F-150 and Wade's plan for tomorrow, side by side on the fridge. He wanted them there so he'd see them first thing in the morning. A reminder. A standard to reach for.

He didn't notice the drawing.

It was pinned lower, at Amelia's eye level, half-hidden behind the lunch menu. A family portrait in crayon on manila paper. It was the kind they did at school, where the teacher writes the kid's name and the date in the corner in careful print. Amelia R., Ms. Patterson's class. Peyton was in the center, tall, with blue scrubs and a careful smile. Kelli was next to her, a riot of yellow curls and a purple dress. Amelia had drawn herself holding Kelli's hand.

Wade was on the far right. Smaller than the others, almost at the edge of the paper, like he'd been added as an afterthought or was in the process of leaving. He was holding a rectangle in his hand. A phone, probably, though it might have been meant as a briefcase. His mouth was a straight line. Everyone else was smiling.

He didn't see it. He was looking at his notecard. The clean lines of his handwriting and the promise of a morning where everything would be different was his only focus. He would try harder, push more, and do the work to be better. He would continue to grind through the resistance. It was what every broker, coach, and conference speaker had told him. This was the only path to the life he wanted.

The problem was effort. It had to be. That's all that got Jon Roberts through the grind of running an auto shop. The alternative is to sit in the question, and the question is unbearable.

Wade turned off the kitchen light. He put the cake in the sink and told himself he'd clean the mess for Peyton in the morning. He climbed the stairs quietly, brushed his teeth in the dark, and slid into bed beside Peyton.

The house lay dark and still. The drawing was on the fridge where it had been for three weeks.

Wade didn't even notice that it almost exactly matched the drawing on the sidewalk outside.

THE INDUSTRY STANDARD

The Monday morning sales meeting at Turner & Associates started at nine sharp. What that really meant was that Sam Turner started talking at nine sharp and he wouldn't stop. But, he worked hard to fill the room with enough enthusiastic energy to power a small generator. Wade slid into his chair near the back with a lukewarm coffee and a knot behind his sternum that had been there since Saturday night, when he'd lain awake staring at the ceiling fan listening to Peyton breathe. All he could think was: is she really sleeping or just done with me?

"Alright, team. New week, new opportunities, new chances to change somebody's life," Sam said. He clapped his hands together at the front of the room, standing behind a podium he didn't need because he never stayed behind it. He was already pacing, already vibrating with the particular energy of a man who had found his calling in the encouragement of others. It didn't seem to register to him that positivity, by itself, doesn't pay anyone's mortgage. "Who's fired up?"

A few voices responded. Jordan Whitfield, near the front, raised his coffee cup without looking up from his phone. Sloan Mills nodded once, already scribbling something in a leather-bound planner that looked like it had been to war and back. When Sam asked again, the room gave him the full performance knowing it had to be done to keep him moving.

"I love it. I love the energy. Now listen, I was at a conference in Nashville last week, and the number one thing I heard from every top producer in that room was the same thing." Sam paused for effect. The room waited. "You. Gotta. Hustle!" He let each word land like it was a revelation instead of the same sentence he'd been saying since Wade got his license. "It's a numbers game, people. Always has been. The agents who are crushing it right now? They're not smarter than you. They're not luckier than you. They're just picking up the phone more than you."

Wade took a sip of his coffee. It tasted like it had been brewed yesterday, as stale as Sam's motivation. He'd heard this rally before. Not this exact version, but close enough. Make more calls. Door knock harder. Farm another neighborhood. Post more content. The advice never changed, only the packaging. Last month it was "double your touchpoints." Before that, "own your mornings." Before that, a guest speaker who sold a $2,000 course on building a personal brand through Instagram Reels and who, Wade later discovered, had closed exactly four transactions the previous year.

He looked around the room. Fifteen agents, most of them newer than Wade, a few of them veterans who attended these meetings the way some people attend church. They came out of habit and a vague hope that something might land differently this time. Their faces held the expression Wade recognized because he wore it himself: a cocktail of caffeine, optimism, and quiet terror that neither was enough.

Sam was still talking. He'd moved on to a whiteboard where he'd written "ACTIVITY = RESULTS" in block letters, underlined twice. "I want everyone in this room to commit to twenty additional contacts this week. Twenty. That's four a day. You can do four a day, right? That's nothing. That's before your second cup of coffee."

A woman in the second row raised her hand. "Contacts meaning calls, or does social media count?"

"Great question," Sam replied. "Everything counts. Calls, texts, DMs, handwritten notes, door knocks — the point is connection. The need is to get in front of people. The more people who know your name, the more people who think of you when they think real estate."

Wade wrote "20 contacts/week" in his notebook, underneath "15 contacts/week" from three weeks ago and "25 contacts/week — MINIMUM" from the month before that. The numbers kept changing. The advice didn't.

Sam wrapped up with a story about an agent in Nashville who went from struggling to closing forty-two transactions in a year by "simply doubling her outreach." The room applauded. Wade applauded too, because that's what you did. He noticed that Sam didn't mention what happened to the agent the year after that. He wondered if she missed birthdays like he did. Those details weren't part of the story. They never were.

The meeting broke at 10:15 AM. Wade was refilling his coffee in the break room when he found the good stuff. The bag Sloan brought from home. She'd given up on the office blend years ago. She told Wade once that if she was going to work as hard as she did, she'd at least enjoy the coffee. The thought of Sloan stating that with such cheerful defiance made him smile. He didn't notice when Jordan appeared beside him.

"Roberts." Jordan leaned against the counter with the easy posture of someone who had never once worried about whether he belonged in a room. He was thirty-five, square-jawed, and wore a sport coat that cost more than Wade's car payment.

Jordan's grandfather's name was on the wall in the lobby. Third-generation top agent. His father, a top producer in his own time, had married into the Turner family. His mother, also a Turner, too was a top producer. When Jordan's grandfather retired, his parents took over ownership and kept the legacy alive. Sam, his uncle, took over from them when they semi-retired a few years back. Jordan was the legacy of that name: embossed, gold-lettered, and completely unavoidable when anyone walked in the door.

"How's the week looking?"

"Getting there," Wade said. "Got a showing this afternoon. Two more Wednesday."

"Three showings. Pretty solid." Jordan nodded slowly, the way a doctor nods when you describe symptoms he's already diagnosed. "I've got twelve lined up. Already confirmed. My assistant's blocking out the week right now."

Wade didn't say anything. There wasn't anything to say. Jordan didn't deliver the number like an insult. That was the thing about Jordan. He delivered it like a midday news report. Like he was reporting a fact about the world that existed whether you liked it or not.

"How bad do you want it, man?" Jordan said, still easy, still casual, still holding his coffee like a prop in a scene he'd rehearsed. "Because I need it. Every morning I wake up and I need it. I think you do too, brother. Ever want some help, you let me know."

Jordan's father had given him a client list of ten thousand names the day he got his license. Wade thought about the assistant Jordan had mentioned, and a second assistant he hadn't mentioned but everyone knew he had. Jordan's marketing budget was funded by a family trust. He thought about the word *need* and how it sounded different coming from someone who'd never had to wonder whether the checking account could cover groceries.

But he didn't say any of that. He said, "Yeah. You're right. I just need to put in more work. I might take you up on that."

Jordan clapped him on the shoulder. "That's the spirit. Hey, you should come to my open house Sunday. Buckhead listing. $1.2 million. Watch how I work the room. You'll pick up some things."

"I'll try," Wade said. It was what he always said. Both of them knew the truth. Wade had his own open house on a $285,000 ranch in Douglasville where the biggest crowd he could expect was two retirees and a nosy neighbor who wanted to confirm their house was indeed better.

Jordan left with a wave, phone already at his ear, already in motion toward whatever the next thing was. Wade stood in the break room holding coffee he no longer wanted and feeling something he couldn't name. It wasn't anger. Jordan hadn't been cruel. Something more like a question forming underwater, still blurry, not yet ready to surface.

Sloan found him at his rented desk twenty minutes later. She materialized the way she always did; mid-sentence, mid-stride, holding her phone in one hand and a protein bar in the other. As if she'd been having a conversation with him that had started somewhere down the hall and only just arrived.

"—and I told them, listen, if you're not available when the client calls, somebody else will be. That's just the reality." She perched on the edge of Wade's desk without asking, which she did with everyone. No one objected because Sloan closed an absurd number of deals every year. Her numbers were the currency that bought her the right to sit wherever she wanted.

"Morning, Sloan." Wade kept his voice even. She wasn't performing for him. He just happened to be in the room.

She didn't wait for the invitation. "Wade, can I ask you something? How quickly do you return calls?"

"Usually within an hour. Sometimes—"

"Within an hour." She shook her head. Not disapprovingly. Sadly, almost. Like a doctor delivering a prognosis. "I return every call within fifteen minutes. Every text within five. My clients know they can reach me any time. Seven in the morning, ten at night, weekends, holidays. That's what it takes."

"Every call?" Wade said. "Even at night? I don't know if Peyt—"

She cut him off. "Especially at night. That's when they're making decisions. That's when they're sitting on the couch with their spouse talking about whether to make an offer. If you're not there in that moment, you've lost them." She took a bite of the protein bar. Her phone buzzed. She glanced at it, typed something with her thumb without breaking eye contact with Wade, and continued. "I had a client call me Christmas morning last year. Christmas morning. His wife was opening presents and he wanted to put in an offer on a lot in Roswell. You know what I did?"

"You took the call."

"I took the call. Wrote the offer. Had it submitted by noon. That was $20,000 commission because I picked up my phone while everyone else was opening presents. Some people just want it bad enough."

Wade looked at Sloan. Really looked at her. He saw the dark half-moons under her eyes that her concealer couldn't quite cover. He saw the way she held her phone like it was a vital organ, something she couldn't be separated from without medical consequence. The protein bar was probably lunch, or what passed for it. Her nails were perfect. Her hair was perfect. Her smile was the practiced kind that arrives on command and doesn't reach the eyes, and he realized he'd never seen the other kind on her.

"Sixty-three closings last year," she said, as if she'd read his hesitation as doubt. "That doesn't happen by accident. That happens because I decided a long time ago that this career was going to be everything. And it is." Her phone buzzed again. She slid off his desk. "Think about it. Fifteen minutes. That's the standard."

She walked away already talking to whoever was on the other end of the call, heels clicking with the mechanical precision of someone who had optimized every minute of her life and eliminated everything that didn't produce a closing.

Wade watched her go and thought, is that what winning looks like? He didn't have an answer. But the fact that the question arrived at all felt like something. He knew, at least, that the way Sloan worked wasn't his answer.

He caught Sam in his office at lunchtime. The door was open. Sam's door was always open, which he called an "open-door policy." In practice it mostly meant Sam used the standing invitation to avoid anything that required sustained focus. Sam made no secret he considered his sole purpose was to be a motivator.

"Sam, you got a minute?"

"Wade! Always. Come in, sit down. How'd the meeting land for you this morning?"

"Good," Wade said, because you said good. "Actually, that's kind of what I wanted to talk about. The calls thing, the numbers game. I'm having some trouble. Is there an automated way to get my calls out and still have some time left—"

"Hey, I hear you," Sam said, leaning back in his chair with the practiced warmth of a man who had perfected the art of gentle disagreement. "And I love that you're thinking about this. But respectfully, you can't automate relationship building. You just have to do it."

Wade waited for the answer to the question he'd asked.

"Here's what I've seen, Wade. In thirty years of this business. The agents who overthink it? They get stuck. They're looking for some magic formula when the formula's right in front of them. Make the calls. Do the work. Stay positive. It'll click." Sam nodded, apparently to himself. "It always clicks. Sometimes it just takes longer than you want."

"Right, but what if—"

"You know what I'd do? Get yourself an accountability partner. Someone to check in with daily. Make sure you're hitting your numbers. Jordan might be a good fit. That boy's got the kind of drive that's contagious."

Wade pictured calling Jordan every morning to report his activity numbers and felt something curl up and die in his chest. "Yeah," he said. "Maybe. He just offered the same thing."

Sam laughed with the bellowing force of a lumberjack. "That boy's a Turner!" When the laugh settled and he saw Wade wasn't sharing the amusement, he continued just as his phone started to ring. "Just keep at it, Wade. You've got the talent. I see it. Now you just need the activity to match. I gotta take this, but get with Jordan and let's circle back."

"Sure," Wade said. He stood up and walked out of Sam's office feeling more alone than when he'd walked in. Sam wasn't unkind. He was never unkind. He just hadn't answered the question. He'd responded with conviction but couldn't explain it in any way that meant something. He was simply convinced that effort was always the answer.

Wade sat alone in his car in the parking lot. Engine off, windows up. He just wanted to stop moving long enough for something to catch up with him.

He pulled his journal from his bag on the passenger seat. The pages were full of showing notes and client addresses. He had scribble an innumerable number of reminders he'd never looked at again, including ones about spending time with Peyton and the girls. He started a list. Everything the industry said to do. Everything Sam and Jordan and Sloan and the conferences and the podcasts and the Instagram gurus said was the path:

Make more calls.

Door knock.

Farm a neighborhood.

Post on social media every day.

Set up Canva templates.

Always be networking, not "working."

Send handwritten notes.

Build a personal brand.

Respond to every lead within five minutes.

Be available 24/7.

Buy online leads.

Follow up until they buy or die.

Always be closing.

Never eat alone.

Your sphere is your goldmine.

Treat every person you meet as a potential client.

He stared at the list. It filled most of a page. Then he went through it with a pen and put a check mark next to everything he was already doing.

He checked almost every line.

The list didn't reveal a gap. That was the thing he couldn't shake. He'd expected to find something missing. One tactic he'd over-looked, one strategy he hadn't tried, the single piece that would explain why he was three years in and still drowning. People like Jordan cruised and people like Sloan sprinted and people like Sam stood at the front of the room and promised that the answer was more of the same.

But there was no missing piece. There was only the same piece, repeated in different fonts at different volumes by people who believed it for different reasons and none of whom had ever stopped to ask whether the piece itself was the problem.

He thought about Kelli. She'd asked him last night, while he was tucking her in, if he'd be home for dinner tomorrow. He'd said "I'll try."

She had looked at him like she already knew what that meant. She knew it from her birthday. For some reason, she decided to love him anyway.

He set down the journal and thought about his father. Jon Roberts. If there was one thing he'd gotten from his old man, it was the habit of writing every thought down in these books. His father worked six days a week at the shop and never missed a game. Not once. Wade had been thinking about that more and more since Peyton's quiet sentence on Kelli's birthday. It sat in him like a stone he couldn't cough up.

His father figured it out. Or at least it looked that way from where Wade sat now, years later, in a parking lot. All he had was a series of checked boxes and nothing to show for any of them.

He didn't know how Jon had done it. He'd always assumed it was a simpler time; fewer demands, a business that ran itself once you got the wrench turning. Maybe that was true. Maybe it wasn't. He didn't have anyone to really ask except his mom, and she never knew much about the actual business.

Wade looked at the list one more time. He didn't have a new answer. The old one, work harder, make more calls, grind until it clicks, still sat in the space where a strategy should be. It wasn't working. If anything, the opposite.

He pressed his eyes closed for a moment. Took a breath. A grown man wasn't supposed to feel this way, and he pushed the feeling down before he started the car. Slowly, he pulled out of the parking lot and drove toward his one-thirty showing. He didn't know what to ask for help with, but the question that wouldn't form itself into words was there in the passenger seat beside him.

Family Legacy

The drive to his mother's house took forty minutes on a Saturday morning, which meant Wade spent forty minutes thinking about all the things he should have been doing instead.

Two follow-up calls he'd promised himself he'd make before noon. A CMA he owed a lead from Thursday. He wasn't even sure the lead was good, but he couldn't afford to let it slip. A Sunday open house he hadn't prepped for. No flyers printed, no signs in the trunk, nothing posted online. The list scrolled through his head the way it always did when he was driving somewhere that wasn't related to a deal. This was the only time it had room to unspool. When he was working he was too busy adding to it to notice how long it had gotten.

He turned off I-20 at the Villa Rica exit and the strip malls fell away to acreage and a Dollar General. A few turns and he'd be on the road his parents lived on for thirty years. Now just his mother's road, but Wade still thought of it as theirs.

The house looked the same. Wade always thought that was the problem. The same brick ranch. The same Bradford pears lining the driveway that his father had planted the year Wade started Little League. The same old mailbox with the hand-painted "ROBERTS" that Jon had lettered himself. He'd said paying someone to write your own name was a waste of money. Everything remained the same. Except the man who'd held it all together was eighteen months gone. The house had the particular stillness of a place that had been built around a lot more people and now only held one.

Wade noticed things he hadn't on his last visit. The gutter over the garage was pulling away from the fascia. The Bradford pears needed trimming, they'd grown wild without his dad's annual assault with the pole saw. The garage door was closed, which it never used to be. His father had kept it open during the day because friendly neighbors sometimes dropped by, and because Jon Roberts was the kind of man who considered a closed garage door a form of unfriendliness.

His mother was waiting on the porch when he pulled up. She looked as he imagined Kelli would have looked on her birthday had he made it home in time for her party. Every car that passed before had personally let her down because it wasn't his. Now that it was, she beamed. She seemed smaller than the last time he'd been back here, or maybe he just hadn't looked carefully enough last time. Grief had not diminished her so much as compressed her. She was still sharp-eyed, still upright. There was just less of her occupying the space, as if the world was pressing on her from all sides.

"You're late," she said, which was how she said hello.

"Traffic on 20."

"Mmhmm." She held the screen door open. The kitchen smelled like coffee and something baking. It always did. Which was either a choice or a habit so old it had become indistinguishable from identity. "I made banana bread. Your father's recipe, which means it tastes like shit."

Wade smiled. His mother's humor had always operated in that register. She didn't curse often. His father hadn't thought it was very Southern of her, so she did it to tease him. She wasn't South-ern, after all, and his father loved that about her. She badly missed having that foil. Wade could see the shadow of it pass across her face when she caught herself being funny with no one to oversell the punchline.

"Happy birthday to Dad," he said quietly, setting his keys on the counter.

She poured him coffee without asking how he took it. "He would have been sixty-four. Can you imagine? Sixty-four. He still thought he was thirty. Moving engine blocks around like they were grocery bags." She shook her head. "Stubborn man."

Wade took the coffee. It was too hot and too strong, the way Jon had always made it. The way she still made it.

"I need your help with the garage," she said. The way she said it without preamble, just the fact of needing, told Wade she'd been holding onto this for a while. She didn't want to ask, but couldn't avoid it anymore. "I can't do it alone. I've tried. I get in there and I just..." She trailed off and wouldn't finish.

"Whatever you need, Mom."

"I need it sorted. What to keep, what to donate." She stopped. The words she couldn't say was throw away. Admitting that some stuff was just garbage meant permanently separating herself from her husband. She wasn't ready for that arithmetic. "Just help me decide."

After an hour or so of bad coffee, good banana bread, and the niceties of talking about Peyton and the girls, Wade made his way to the garage.

It still smelled like motor oil, metal shavings, and the faint sweetness of old wood. The smells were stale but they were still very real. This was his father's real office. The shop on Highway

61 was where the work happened. This two-car garage with its pegboard walls and fluorescent lights and oil-stained concrete floor was where Jon Roberts had been most himself.

Wade's mother stood in the doorway for a moment, then said, "I'll be inside," and left him there. He understood. She'd gotten him to the threshold. The rest was his.

The tools weren't just organized. They were catalogued with devotion. One out of place would have been a moral violation. Wrenches graduated by size on the pegboard, separated by metric and imperial, each one hanging from its own labeled hook. Socket sets in foam-lined cases, the foam cut to fit each piece so that a missing socket announced itself as a gap. Screwdrivers in a wall-mounted rack, flathead, Phillips, Torx, arranged not alphabetically but by frequency of use. A system only Jon would have devised and only Jon would have followed.

Wade ran his fingers along the workbench. A thick layer of dust had settled over everything, softening the edges. The space felt like a museum exhibit of someone's life rather than the life itself. He found a Braves cap hanging from a nail, sun-faded, sweat-stained, the bill curved into a permanent arc from years of Jon pulling it on and off. Wade held it for a moment. Set it back.

He started with the obvious things. A box of rags, stiff with age. Cans of brake cleaner and WD-40 lined up like soldiers. A tool chest his father had bought in 1994 and maintained with the same care other men gave their cars. Inside the chest, more tools. Beneath the tools, service manuals, thick, greasy-cornered things with titles like Repair Manual: Ford F-150, 1993–2004 and GM Full-Size Trucks, 1988–1998.

For a few hours, he sorted and organized what was already sorted and organized. Except, his purpose was different and his father's methods didn't apply anymore. When he'd packed away tools and disposed of old unnecessary things, he saw a box on the shelf above the workbench between a can of hand cleaner and a stock of shop rags. He pulled it down. Inside, five composition books—his father's old journals.

These were the kind with the black-and-white marbled covers Wade associated with middle school. They were worn but not damaged. The first one had a date written on the inside cover in Jon's handwriting, which was neater than you'd expect from a man whose fingers were permanently creased with grease: Started January 2003.

Wade opened it.

The entries weren't what he expected. These were entirely different from the notebook Jon Roberts always had with operational notes. Wade just assumed that all his father's journals would be a log of jobs. Brake pads replaced. Timing belts installed. Transmissions rebuilt. And that information was there, written in his father's careful hand on the left side of each page.

Still, these journals were something else entirely.

Weber, Bill — '98 Camry, 180K miles. Mentioned daughter's college graduation next month. Reminded him about the brake job but told him it could wait. Nothing urgent. Family first. He nearly cried. Told me he's been worried about paying for the ceremony and the car repair in the same month. Told him to bring it in July. What's another few weeks on brakes that are worn but safe?

Wade read the entry twice. Then he turned to a page near the back of the journal.

Simmons, Deborah — '02 Accord. Husband just lost his job. She's driving on a tire that needs replacing but only came in for an oil change because that's what she could afford. Put the tire on and charged her for the oil change. She doesn't need to know. She needs to know her car is safe.

Then, in a different color pen: *Deb noticed the tire. Brought in some money with her husband and insisted I take it.*

Page after page. Customer after customer. Not just their cars but their lives, documented with the same attention and precision Jon gave his tools. He'd written down the names of customers' children. Their health concerns. Their worries. He'd noted when someone seemed stressed, when someone mentioned a job change, when someone's kid made the travel team or got into trouble at school.

One entry stopped Wade cold.

Gabaldon, Esteban — fleet maintenance, quarterly. Brought tamales from his mother's recipe for the shop. Told me his manufacturing contacts are struggling. Recession hitting the suppliers hard. I mentioned we were slow too. He sent seven of his people to us the next week. Seven. Didn't ask for anything. Just said good mechanics are hard to find and he wanted to make sure we stayed open. Just a damn good man. I miss having him around.

Wade sat on the stool beside the workbench and kept reading. His own notepads were random, stream-of-consciousness. His dad's were chronicles of people's lives.

He lost track of time. He'd find an entry, then remember seeing the same name in another notebook and try to piece together the chronology. It was like reading the history of a small town. Stories that connected him with people he'd never known but whose lives Jon had documented with an intimacy that felt almost private.

The fluorescent light buzzed overhead. The smell of oil hung in the air. His father's handwriting filled page after page with the stories of men, women, and children who meant more than a vehicle to him.

It wasn't just that Jon had been kind to his customers. Plenty of people were kind. It was that Jon had been deliberate about it. The journals weren't sentimental. They were operational. Jon used the notes. An entry from March would reference a detail from September:

Asked about Linda's hip surgery. She mentioned it in the fall. Recovery went well. Brought her flowers from the garden.

He wasn't just tracking what people's cars needed. He was tracking what their drivers needed, and he'd built his record-keeping around it.

There was a pattern in entry after entry. Jon had made choices that sacrificed short-term revenue for something else. He'd delayed jobs that weren't urgent so customers could breathe. He'd done extra work he didn't charge for. He'd turned away business he could have taken. And the result was clear. Wade could trace it through the journals like a river finding its course.

Customers always came back. Always. They came back and they brought people with them. They stayed for decades, not because Jon was the cheapest mechanic or the fastest. He was the one who remembered their daughter's graduation. He wanted to know about their husband's job. He put on a desperately needed tire without being asked because it was the right thing to do. He'd decided that doing the right thing was the business.

Wade closed the journal. His hands were shaking slightly. Not from cold.

He'd spent three years trying to honor his father's memory by grinding. By working sixty-hour weeks. By never saying no to an opportunity. By treating every moment away from work as a moment wasted, because that's what providers did. They provided, relentlessly. His father had worked six days a week for decades. That was the story Wade had told himself. That was the legacy he was trying to live up to.

The journals told a different story.

His mother appeared in the garage doorway with two mugs of coffee. She could read Wade's face the same way he'd been reading the journals. She set a mug on the workbench and wrapped both hands around her own.

"You found the journals," she said. Not a question.

"Did you know about these?"

"Of course I knew. He kept every single one of them. I used to tease him about it. Assumed he was writing a novel about carburetors."

"They're not about carburetors."

"No," she said. "They're not. And thank the good lord. His mechanics, the ones who bought the place, paid a few high schoolers for a whole summer just to enter every note from every book into their computers. Brought them all back to me as soon as they were done. I suppose I forgot about these specific ones."

Wade looked back at the journals he had in front of him. "He knew all of them. Every customer. Their families, their problems, what was going on in their lives. He wrote it all down."

His mother took a sip of coffee. "Your father believed that if you're going to do something for someone, you should know who they are first. Not just what their car needs. Who they are." She said it simply, without emphasis, the way you state something you've never had reason to question. "He used to say the car was just the reason they walked in the door. What kept them in the waiting room was the handshake."

Wade thought about his own client interactions. The hurried phone calls. The showing appointments he rushed through to get to the next one. The names he forgot, the details he never asked about. The follow-ups that fell through the cracks because there were always more cracks than follow-ups. He thought about Sloan answering calls on Christmas morning. He thought about Sam preaching volume from a podium. He thought about his own journal in the car, its pages full of scratch marks that had meant something urgent when he wrote them and nothing at all by Thursday.

"Mom, how did he do it?"

"Do what?"

"Work six days a week and still be...around. He never missed a game. Not one. Every Saturday tournament, every weeknight game under the lights. He was there. Third row behind the home dugout, grease still under his fingernails because he came straight from the shop. How?"

She looked at him over the rim of her mug, and something passed across her face. The particular tenderness of someone watching you arrive at a question they've been waiting for you to ask.

"He decided," she said.

Wade waited.

"That's all there was to it. He decided that nothing was more important than being there at those moments. Not a brake job, not a fleet contract, not money. He planned his days around us. If a customer needed something done and it conflicted with your schedule, he told them the truth. My son has a game, I'll get to it tomorrow. It's date night, and I need to be out of here early. Those kind of things. And you know what happened?"

Wade waited.

"Not a single customer left. Not one. Because they had families too. They understood. And they respected him more for it, not less." She paused. "Work can wait. Family can't. He said that so often it was practically tattooed on him."

Wade stared at his coffee. The surface trembled slightly and he realized it was his hand. He thought about Kelli asking if he'd be home for dinner. He thought about the patience in her five-year-old voice. The kind that shouldn't exist in a five-year-old, the kind that gets learned from disappointment.

"I've been trying to be like him," Wade said quietly. "I thought...I thought what he taught me was that you work hard. That you show up every day and you grind and you don't complain and that's how you take care of your family."

His mother set her mug down. "Wade. Your father was the hardest-working man I ever knew. I just don't think you saw what he actually worked on. He worked every day to be your father. He knew exactly what he was doing and why he was doing it. Being a mechanic came naturally to him. He could fix anything. It took a lot of work for him to be here with us. Eventually, he just said the cost of business sometimes is being at a baseball game."

The garage was quiet. The fluorescent light buzzed. Somewhere outside, a mockingbird was working through its repertoire. Cycling through stolen songs with the persistence of a creature that didn't know any of them were borrowed.

"I'm not sure I know the difference," Wade said.

"I know," she said. Gently, without judgment. She watched her son misread his father's life and waited, without pressure, for him to notice. He didn't know if that was worse or better than what he'd expected from her today. Then, it dawned on him why his mom hadn't cleaned out the garage after all. She needed her son to discover his father on his own.

Wade drove home with the journals on the passenger seat. All five of them, plus an entire trunk full of boxes his mother had pulled from storage. His journal remained on the seat but wasn't at all the same thing. Two entirely different languages, describing two entirely different understandings of what it meant to work.

Wade's journal said: Do more. Be more available. Make more calls. The answer is volume. His father's words said something else, but Wade couldn't articulate what, exactly. His father hadn't out-hustled anyone. He'd been something more specific and more deliberate. The result was a business and a customer base that spanned decades, their stories woven together with his.

Then his thoughts drifted to Peyton. *I'm not asking you to choose between your career and your family. You have to figure out how to have both. Because right now, you don't have either.* She'd said it without raising her voice. At the time it had sounded like disappointment.

Sitting here now, with his father's journals beside him, it sounded like something else. It sounded like exactly what his mother had described: a decision. Peyton wasn't asking him to choose between two things. She was asking him to decide what kind of person he was going to be.

His father had decided, and Wade loved him for it. Jon Roberts, with his grease-stained hands and his composition journals and his six-day weeks that still left room for every game, had done exactly that. Why couldn't he? Wade had spent three years staring at the wrong half of his father's legacy.

He pulled into his driveway. Through the window he could see Peyton at the counter. He didn't go inside right away. He sat with the engine off and his hands on the wheel and the journals on the seat beside him. In those journals was the record of a man who had figured something out; what to protect, what to let go, what to ignore. Wade didn't know the formula yet. But he could see the product in that window.

When he did walk in, he could see Kelli intensely concentrating on stirring something in a bowl as if she were performing surgery. She stood on a step stool, and still she needed to stretch on the tips of her toes. Amelia was at the kitchen table, drawing. A Saturday evening, ordinary and unremarkable. At that exact moment, Wade felt something shift. It was small, but it was noticeable.

Kelli looked up from her bowl. Batter on her chin, flour on her shirt. "Daddy! We're making cookies. Mama said you might be too tired, but I saved you the spoon."

Wade took the spoon. He paused for a second, which caught Amelia's attention, too. Then, with cartoonish exaggeration, he said, "Well, good, because I am only going to eat cookie dough and none of y'all are gonna stop me!"

Kelli squealed. Amelia smiled and went back to her drawing. Even Peyton allowed herself a soft smile.

Wade's mind and body were in the same place. He didn't pull out his phone. He didn't sit down at the table to open his computer. He didn't even rush to read more of his father's journals.

He just ate cookie dough that tasted better than any meal in recent memory.

CHANCE ENCOUNTER

The continuing education classroom smelled like lavender. Wade assumed the building managers pumped it through the vents to manufacture calm. He could think of worse things, given what he was being asked to endure for this professional obligation. The forty-five minutes he'd spent driving here on a Saturday morning was the real pain. He could have spent his time with the girls, a Saturday Peyton hadn't commented on when he mentioned it the night before. That was how she communicated disappointment now, through the things she chose not to say.

The class was called Legal Updates and Risk Management: What Every Georgia Agent Needs to Know. It was exactly as riveting as the title suggested. A man in a gray suit stood at the front of the room reading from slides. The monotone drawl of his voice added to the overwhelming number of words on each slide. Even the lavender was working against Wade, as the calming effect was putting him in a trance.

Wade sat in the third row pretending to take notes, but he spent a good portion of the time just doodling. His phone was supposed to be off, so games were out. When his middle school art skills hit the limit, and any attempt at actual engagement couldn't be sustained, he would let his mind drift back to his father's journals. He'd been turning over those journals for weeks now.

He'd been reading them every night after the girls went to bed. Not all at once. Just a few pages at a time, the way you'd read letters from someone you were only beginning to understand. Each entry pulled him deeper into a version of his father he hadn't known existed. Jon Roberts, the man Wade had eulogized as "the hardest worker I ever knew," had been something else entirely. Something more precise. Wade kept circling back to the same word, testing it against what he was reading: deliberate. Not just hardworking. Deliberate about where the work went and what it was for.

But knowing that didn't help Wade figure out what to do with it. The crack in his thinking, the one his mother had widened with her quiet correction in the garage, was still just a crack. Light came through it, but he couldn't see what was on the other side.

When Wade snapped back to the room, the man in the gray suit was talking about disclosure requirements. Something about seller's property condition statements and the seventeen ways you could accidentally expose yourself to a lawsuit. Wade wrote *SPDS* in his notebook and underlined it. He made it important so he had something to underline. The act of underlining gave him something to do with the restlessness that had been building since he sat down.

He looked around the room. Forty-odd agents. Some of them stared at their phones under the tables, as mentally present as he was. Others used their notebooks as sketchpads, same as him. The agent directly in front of him appeared to have legitimate gallery-quality work going on. A few agents actually paid attention. Wade assumed those were the newer ones. They still believed that absorbing enough information would eventually produce competence. He'd been one of them a few years ago. Now he sat in the third row unable to tell whether the information itself was the problem or the fact that none of it told him what to do first.

What to do first. That was the question he couldn't get away from. Not what to do. He had a list for that, longer than his days. But what to do first. He couldn't narrow that down. If he made the wrong choice of where to begin, he could set himself back further. If he started to make the right changes, he wasn't sure he would stick with them. Even his father's journals hadn't made that point clear.

The morning session broke at noon. The man in the gray suit invited everyone to networking during lunch. Wade stood up and stretched. He was just going to leave. He had his hours logged. He could drive home and get some work done. He'd maybe make it back before Kelli's nap ended. That was the responsible thing. Any other version of Wade from the past three years would have done so without hesitation.

But he was afraid of missing something. This new thread of thinking — *where do I start?* — had him curious. The afternoon was vaguely about connecting business and consumer protection, so it might be a class that could point him in the right direction. So he stayed.

The lunch setup was standard: sandwich trays, canned sodas in a cooler, and a room full of agents performing the particular theater of professional networking. Business cards exchanged as a pleasantry. Conversations that started with vague generalities and ended with someone scanning the room for a more useful target. The energy was kinetic and desperate. The way it always was when you put forty independent contractors who all did the same thing in a room and told them to connect.

Wade took a turkey sandwich and a soda and found a seat near the windows. He didn't feel like networking. He didn't feel like performing enthusiasm or comparing transaction counts. He had no patience for someone's latest marketing strategy that was really just every other marketing strategy with a different name. He wanted to sit still by himself.

That's when he saw her.

She was sitting two tables over, by herself, eating a sandwich and reading a book. She just read an actual book and ate in peace. Around her, the room buzzed with frenetic movement. Agents were reflexively checking their phones for something they missed. Every conversation was a contest between two people flexing their competitive edge. And in the middle of it; this woman and her book.

It took a moment, but Wade recognized her. Terry Bass. He'd heard her speak at a regional conference a year or two back. Her presentation on something she called "strategic client selection". He attended because it fell between a session on Instagram Reels and one on adapting cold-calling to the new age of AI. He needed the break from being talked at. The topic had sounded different enough to be worth checking out.

He remembered dismissing it. She'd talked about choosing your clients instead of chasing them. About how time was worth nothing until you were actually paid for it. Called her methods something like constraint-based thinking. Wade had sat in the back thinking: easy to say when you've already made it. He couldn't afford to be selective when he was making so little and trying to work so hard. He'd walked out before the Q&A.

Now he was two tables away from her. Watching her read without any awareness of or interest in what was happening around her. He felt something pull him over to try and speak with her. Even though he told himself she clearly didn't want to be bothered, he mustered the courage to interrupt her momentary zen.

He thought about what his father would do here. He did have an ability to just talk with people. If Jon would approach a chance conversation with gusto, Wade told himself that maybe this was the place to start.

Before he could talk himself out of it, Wade picked up his lunch and walked over.

"Hi. Terry, right? Can I sit with you?"

She looked up from her book. Her eyes were calm and faintly amused. The look of someone prepared for the small talk that was apparently about to arrive.

"Seat's all yours," she said.

Wade sat down and immediately didn't know what to say. Purpose had carried him to the table. Now that he was here, the purpose had evaporated and left behind a man with a turkey sandwich and no opening line.

"My name is Wade Roberts. I heard you speak at the regional conference last year. The strategic client selection talk."

"Yes, I remember that talk," Terry chuckled. "Small room. A few people left before I finished." She said it without bitterness, but still looked directly at Wade when she said that. Then, smiled and winked.

Wade sheepishly said, "You remember that?"

"I pay attention to who's in a room. It's an important skill for me," Terry said. She closed her book and set it on the table, cover down. He caught a glimpse of the title, something about scaling he didn't recognize. "Where do you call home these days, Wade?"

"Turner and Associates," Wade replied.

Terry chuckled again. "No, I mean where do you live. But since you brought it up. How long have you been with Sam?"

"Right," Wade said. "Dallas. I live over in Dallas with my family. Been with Sam three years."

"How's that going? The working with Sam, since you brought it up."

It was a simple question. People asked it all the time. How's business, how's the market, how are things going. The answer was always a version of great, busy, can't complain. That was the script, the mask you wore in a profession where admitting you were struggling felt like bleeding in shark-infested waters.

Wade opened his mouth. He meant to deliver a script. He hesitated, and what came out instead surprised him.

"Honestly? I don't know."

Terry just waited for what he was going to say next. His father's journals waited between entries in the same way. It recorded the conversation, and then simply waited for the next time he'd meet that client. Open, patient, leaving space for whatever was going to come.

"I'm working sixty hours a week. Making every call. Doing everything Sam tells me to do. I have a list, an ongoing and never-ending list. I've checked off every box on it. And I'm still..." He paused. The word that wanted to come out was drowning, but he'd never said it out loud to another agent. Barely to himself. "I'm not where I thought I'd be."

"Where did you think you'd be?" Terry asked. She leaned in to hear the answer.

"I don't know. Further? Making enough that my wife doesn't have to work so hard. Home for dinner more. Not feeling like I'm running on a treadmill someone keeps tilting steeper." He stopped. He'd said more than he intended. The words had come out with the particular momentum of things compressed too long.

Terry nodded slowly. A prolonged silence settled between them when he didn't continue.

"Can I ask you a question?" she said.

"Sure."

"What's your constraint?"

Wade looked at her. "My what?"

"Your constraint. The one thing that's actually limiting your business right now. Not your list. It might be on the list, but it's not the entire list. If you could only fix one problem, the one that would unlock everything else, what would it be?"

He didn't know how to answer.

"I mean... There are a lot of things. Leads are expensive and they don't convert. My follow-up is a mess. I don't have a system for... anything, really. I'm spending half my time driving to showings that go nowhere. Sam wants me making twenty more contacts a week, but I'm already—"

"That's five things," Terry said. Gently. The way you'd correct a child's math without making them feel bad about the mistake. "And I'd bet you could list ten more if I let you keep going."

"Probably twenty."

"Right. So let me ask it differently. When everything is a problem, what's actually the problem?"

Wade stared at her. The sandwich in his hand had been forgotten. The room receded. The ambient chatter, the anxious movements, the business card exchange all of it faded away.

"I don't... I'm not sure I understand the question."

"That's a good place to start." Terry took a sip of her drink. "Most people in this room could give you the same list you just gave me. Leads, follow-up, systems, time. Everyone has the same problems. But here's the thing about trying to fix every problem on your list. You're spreading your energy across twenty problems, which means none of them get enough attention to move. When everything is the problem, nothing is the problem. You're just not looking at the right thing."

The sentence landed somewhere Wade wasn't expecting. He knew what she meant, even if he couldn't fully articulate it. It didn't land the way tactical advice landed. It landed in the same place his father's journals pressed. Somewhere below the reasoning, in the part that recognized truth before he could explain why.

"So how do I figure out which one it is?" he asked.

Terry smiled. Not the practiced smile of professional nicety, but the smile of someone who has heard this question before and knows that the asking of it is itself the answer to a different question. "That's the right question. Most people skip straight to the answer they already had before they started asking."

His phone rang.

Wade glanced at the screen. Sam Turner. He felt the reflex before the thought. The immediate pull to answer. The Pavlovian urgency that three years in real estate had welded to the sound of a ringing phone. Every call could be business. Every missed call could be a lost deal. Sloan's voice in his head: If you're not there at that moment, you've lost them.

"Sorry," he said to Terry. "I should — it could be important. It's Sam."

"Please. Go ahead."

He answered. Sam's voice came through with its usual breathless enthusiasm, which made everything sound like a three-alarm blaze. "Wade! Hey, quick thing. I know you're probably at lunch right now. The Jensons want to change the time they look at those listings you gave them from 2 o'clock to 3. Called the office looking for you because they couldn't reach your cell. Can you make that work? Also, I've got a lead I want to pass your way. Guy from the website. Says he's looking in Douglasville. I don't know how serious he was, but anyone asking is serious, right?"

Wade handled it. Confirmed the time change. Took down the lead's name and number. Said "thanks, Sam" in the way that meant goodbye.

When he looked up, Terry was watching him with an expression he couldn't read. Not judgment. Not sympathy. Something like clinical interest. The way a doctor watches you cross a room when you've come in complaining about your back.

"What's new on the list?" she asked.

"Yeah, a change to a showing and a lead."

"That's what those calls always are. The day gets rearranged by someone else's schedule, a new task gets added to the pile, and you spend the rest of the afternoon reacting instead of doing what you'd planned." She paused. "That's a symptom. Not the constraint itself, but a symptom of it."

Wade sat back. "A symptom of what?"

"Your time disappears because you haven't decided what it's actually for. When you don't know what the main thing is, everything becomes the main thing. Every call is urgent. Every lead is important. Every showing is worth rearranging your day for. And at the end of the week, you've been busy but can't actually point to what you accomplished. Sound familiar?"

Wade thought about his notepad in the car. Every box checked. No progress. Then he thought about the journals on his nightstand. The last entry he'd read was about a customer his father had told to bring his car in next month because family came first. Jon did not treat every opportunity as urgent. He treated the important things as important and let the rest wait. His customers respected him more for it, not less.

"You're describing my entire career," Wade said. He meant it to sound like a joke. It didn't.

Terry reached into her bag and pulled out a business card. Plain white. Her name and phone number. No tagline, no photo, no Your Dream Home Awaits. Nothing trying to convince you of anything. Just a name and a way to reach her.

"If you ever want to think about that more carefully," she said, "call me."

Wade took the card. It was lighter than he expected. That was an absurd thing to notice about a business card, but he noticed it anyway. "What would that look like? Thinking about it more carefully?"

"I don't know yet. That depends on what you're willing to question." She picked up her book. "It was good to meet you, Wade."

"You too." He paused. "Can I ask, what are you reading?"

She held up the cover. It's Not Luck, by Eliyahu Goldratt. "A book about a corporate executive trying to save his companies from being sold. Not exactly beach reading, but the thinking in it changed my life." She said it simply, without salesmanship, the way you'd mention a road that you enjoyed a leisurely cruise on.

Wade had never heard of it. He thought he might like to read it, but his mental cabinet was already overflowing with recommendations and tactics and tools he meant to look into and rarely did. Something about the way she'd said the thinking in it changed her life stuck differently, though. She said it with conviction, not performance.

The afternoon session started at one. A different presenter, a woman teaching changes to the buyer-broker agreement. The room settled into the polite attention of people who needed hours and were willing to endure anything to get them. Wade was a bit annoyed at this representing "business and consumer protection." But, he spent the three hours pondering Terry's question.

What's your constraint?

He wrote it at the top of his notepad. He stared at it through most of the class. The question had dropped like a stone in still water. He wanted to stay with the ripples before they faded.

He kept trying to answer it and kept hitting the same wall he'd hit at the table with Terry. Everything was the problem. Leads, time, systems, follow-up, money, knowledge, direction. He could list twenty things that were broken and not identify the one thing underneath them all.

But that was what she'd said, wasn't it? That spreading your energy across every broken thing meant nothing got enough attention to change. That the constraint, the one thing limiting everything else, was right there in the noise, if he could learn to see it.

His thoughts moved to the garage again. His father ran a shop on notebooks and served his people so well that they brought others. He organized his work deliberately around people.

Then Terry, reading her book while the room buzzed with networking panic. She'd chosen what her lunch hour was for. She hadn't avoided everyone. She'd let Wade sit down and talk.

Then, inevitably, Peyton. Her quiet, direct sentence. Her ICU shifts. For her, she and her nurses had to decide what to act on first and let everything else wait. She did that every shift. Decided what mattered most. Acted on that. Let the rest hold.

Three different people. Three versions of the same unnamed idea. When everything is the problem, nothing is. You're just not looking at the right thing.

For the first time, he had a question. Not a checklist. Not a framework. Not five steps he could implement Monday morning. Just a question, bare and unresolved, sitting in the space where the old certainties used to be.

What is my constraint?

The afternoon session ended at four. Terry's business card was in his pocket. The sun was low enough to throw long shadows across the asphalt. The October air had the first edge of a Georgia autumn, not cold yet, but carrying a promise that something was about to change.

He sat in the driver's seat and didn't start the engine. On the seat beside him, his journal. At home on his nightstand, his father's journals. In his pocket, a card from a woman who'd asked him a question no one in three years of real estate had thought to ask.

His father's notebooks had planted a seed. Terry Bass had just watered it.

Wade started the car and drove home. Tonight, he made it in time for dinner.

ANOTHER WAY

Three days.

That's how long Terry's business card sat on Wade's nightstand before he even picked it up. It hadn't moved from where it was propped against his father's journals. Plain white. Terry Bass. A phone number. No tagline, no headshot, no promise. Just a name and a way to reach a woman who'd asked him a question that burrowed into his thinking and wouldn't come out.

He picked it up Tuesday morning. Set it back. Picked it up again Wednesday night after the girls were in bed, Peyton reading quietly on the couch, and held it between his fingers like a coin he was deciding whether to spend.

He thought about calling. Thought about what he'd say. Thought about what she'd say back. Convinced himself she had a coaching pitch waiting. Some consulting package, monthly mentorship, a "no obligation" fee that somehow always became an obligation. Probably learning modules and a private Facebook group where agents posted motivational quotes and screenshots of their latest win. He'd almost signed up for three different versions of that kind of program over the past year. He'd stopped each time he ran the math.

Thursday morning he called.

She picked up on the second ring. That shouldn't have surprised him, but it did. Most agents he knew either answered immediately, like Sloan, or not at all. Terry's second-ring answer had a different quality. Unhurried. Like she'd been doing something, looked at her phone, decided to answer, and done so. No breathlessness, no background noise, no sense of multitasking.

"This is Terry."

"Hey, Terry. It's Wade Roberts. We talked at the CE class on Saturday."

"Wade. I had a feeling it was you." She left a beat of silence. Most people felt compelled to fill it immediately. Terry let it sit. "How can I help?"

He'd rehearsed something. A version of casual professional outreach, something about following up on our conversation that sounded like an email subject line. What came out instead was closer to the truth.

"I've been thinking about what you said. The constraint thing. I keep trying to answer it and I can't, and the fact that I can't is... I don't know. I can't stop thinking about it."

Silence again. The good kind. The kind that meant someone was listening.

"Good," Terry said.

"Good?"

"Most people hear that question and either answer it immediately or never think about it again. If they answer it immediately, they won't investigate it. If they never think about it, same result. The fact that it's still with you means it landed in the right place." A pause. "What are you doing next Tuesday morning?"

"I've got a showing at noon. Before that I was going to make calls."

"Come shadow me instead. Eight-thirty. I'll text you the address." She said it the way you'd give directions to a restaurant.

They were clear and matter-of-fact. "See what I do. Then decide if you want to understand it."

Wade waited for the rest. The price. The terms. The part where generosity became a transaction.

"That's it?" he said.

"That's it."

"No, I mean, what does it cost?"

"A morning." He could hear something in her voice. Not quite amusement, but close. She'd had this conversation before and found the question both predictable and telling. "What's one more when you've spent a couple years striking out?"

He didn't have an answer for that. He said yes and hung up. He held the phone and sat with what he felt. Something he hadn't felt in a long time. Not hope exactly. He almost resented the fact that it was anything at all. Nothing was working. Why would this be different?

On Tuesday morning he drove to the address Terry had texted. He didn't know what to expect, so he'd defaulted to what he knew. Something like Sam's office: a brokerage bullpen with motivational posters, ringing phones, and the frenetic energy of people performing urgency. Or maybe a sleeker version like Jordan's setup: Italian leather and recessed lighting, the aesthetic of success rather than the chaos of it. Either way, he expected some version of the treadmill. More than a few transactions in a year meant chaos. Whether the chaos was better-dressed or more efficiently managed, it was still chaos.

The address led him to a small office park in Kennesaw. Single-story buildings, landscaped but not flashy. Her suite was at the end. A glass door with her name on it and nothing else. No "TEAM TERRY" branding. No transaction count on the window.

No photo of herself shaking hands with a mayor or holding an oversized check.

He walked in at 8:28 and stopped.

Quiet.

Not just the absence of noise. An actual quality to the space. The kind Wade associated with libraries or therapists' offices, designed to let your nervous system stand down. The front area held a small desk with a computer, a potted plant that was alive rather than silk, and a single framed photograph of a girl in a swimming cap, grinning with water streaming down her face.

What it didn't have was just as noticeable. No stacks of paper. No whiteboard covered in transaction pipelines. No sticky notes wallpapering the edges of a monitor. Everything had a place and a purpose. This was not the office of people performing busyness.

Terry came out of the back with two mugs of coffee. She was dressed simply: slacks, a navy blouse, reading glasses pushed up on her head. She moved with the same unhurried quality Wade had noticed at the CE class. It struck him again how alien it looked in someone who did what they did for a living.

"You're here," she said, smiling. She handed him a mug. "That's a good sign."

"You said eight-thirty."

"I said eight-thirty. You're here at eight twenty-eight. In my experience, agents who show up on time are serious. The ones looking for a shortcut arrive late." She took a sip of her coffee. "Come on. I'll show you how a Tuesday works."

She sat at her desk and pulled up something on her screen. A single page that looked like it had been prepared before she arrived. Wade stood behind her, holding his coffee, trying not to hover. The page was clean: a short list of names with notes beside each one, a calendar view of the day's appointments, and a set of bullet points under a header that read Today's Focus.

"My system prepares this every morning," Terry said. "It pulls from my client database, my calendar, and my follow-up sequences, and gives me a summary of who needs attention, what's on the schedule, and what the one or two priority items are for the day."

"Your system?" Wade asked. He didn't know what that meant. CRM? An assistant? He looked around for evidence of another person.

"That's not the most important part. We'll get to it another time." She scrolled through the briefing the way a pilot scans a pre-flight checklist. Terry didn't read every word, but confirmed the things she expected to see were where she expected them. The whole review took three minutes. "Okay. Three video messages first."

She opened her phone, consulted the briefing, and recorded the first video. Wade watched. It was personal. She addressed a specific client by name, referenced only their situation, nothing scripted. No template. No mass message. She looked directly into the camera and spoke directly to the recipient. Wade had the distinct sense she was saying: I see you. I heard you. I want to help you.

She did three of these. Different clients, different situations. One was a past buyer whose anniversary of purchase was coming up. One was a seller whose listing had been on the market for three weeks. Terry gave a brief update on showing feedback and what she was adjusting in the marketing. The third was a referral source, a mortgage broker, thanking him for a smooth closing and asking about a mutual client.

Nine minutes total. Three videos. Three relationships tended.

Wade thought about his own follow-up. The stack of business cards from networking events, rubber-banded in his desk drawer. The CRM that pinged him with "follow up with lead" reminders he swiped away because he didn't remember who the lead was or what they'd talked about. The low-grade guilt he carried about the people he'd met and then lost in the noise of trying to meet more people.

"How do you know what to say to each of them?" he asked.

"My system tracks it. Every conversation, every detail, every important date. When I sit down in the morning, I'm not starting from scratch." She explained a few technical details and hiring a VA who helped set up and manage most of the processes. But Wade couldn't hold onto the specifics. He was still watching the videos in his head.

"Nine-fifteen," Terry said. "Seller call."

The seller call was different from any Wade had witnessed. He'd listened to plenty of prospecting calls. Sam's office ran a call session every Tuesday where agents sat in a room and dialed expired listings from a shared list. They read from scripts that started with "Hi, I noticed your home was recently on the market..." and ended, usually, with a dial tone. Wade had done hundreds of those calls. They felt like throwing darts blindfolded in a dark room and being told the problem was that you weren't throwing enough darts.

Terry's call was to one person. A woman named Diane whose mother had died. She needed to sell the family home, but she wasn't ready yet. Terry mentioned the two previous times they'd spoken. Wade could tell from the ease of the conversation that Terry had been looking forward to it.

Terry didn't sell. She didn't pitch. She asked Diane how she was doing with the estate process. She asked whether Diane's brother had come around on the timing question they'd discussed last month. She mentioned, casually, that the market in Diane's mother's neighborhood had shifted slightly and that waiting another month or two wouldn't hurt. Might actually help. She told Diane the real estate transaction didn't need to add to the difficulty of what she was already carrying.

The call lasted twelve minutes. When she hung up, Wade said, "You told her to wait."

"I told her the truth. Her market's trending up. Her emotional readiness isn't there yet. Pushing her to list now would get me a commission sooner and get her a worse outcome." Terry refilled her coffee. "She'll list in about six weeks. Maybe eight. And when she does, she'll list with me, because I'm the one who told her not to rush."

"But what if she doesn't? What if someone else gets to her first?"

Terry looked at him with an expression Wade would come to recognize. The curious look of someone who'd heard a question that revealed more about the asker than the subject.

"Who's going to get to her? The home isn't on the market. Nobody knows about it except Diane, her brother, and me. I'm the only agent in the picture. If Diane's brother is talking to another agent and they are a better fit, then good. The goal is still accomplished." She paused. "More than that, Diane and I have grown close. She doesn't need a real estate agent right now. She needs a friend."

Wade opened his mouth and closed it. The logic was clean. He felt embarrassed he'd questioned it at all.

"Ten-thirty," Terry said. "Showing."

The showing was in a neighborhood Wade knew, a subdivision off Barrett Parkway where the houses ran mid-400s and the lots backed up to a greenway. Terry's buyers, a couple in their early thirties, met them in the driveway. They were relaxed in a way Wade's buyers never seemed to be. No jittery energy. No sense that they were being managed through a process they didn't understand.

Wade understood why within minutes. They already knew the house. Terry's system had sent them a detailed packet. Not just the MLS listing, but a market comparison, school information, commute analysis, and a note about the HOA's recent assessment history. They'd reviewed it. Their questions were specific and informed, not the scattered confusion of people drowning in options.

Terry showed the house the way she did everything else. No rush. She pointed out what mattered and didn't oversell what didn't. When the wife asked about the water stain on the basement ceiling, Terry said, "That's worth investigating before you make an offer. I'd recommend an inspection with someone who specializes in water intrusion. I have a name for you." She didn't minimize it. She didn't suggest using it as leverage. She treated the question like it deserved a real answer. The couple's trust, already evident when they arrived, deepened visibly.

The showing took thirty minutes. Afterward, in the driveway, the husband shook Terry's hand. "We want to think about it tonight. We'll call you tomorrow."

"Take your time," Terry said. "This is a big decision. If it's right, it'll still be right in the morning."

They drove off. Wade stood in the driveway with his hands in his pockets, doing math in his head that nobody had asked him to do.

"Your buyers were already prepared before they walked in," he said.

"That's the point. My system handles the market analysis, the packet, the scheduling — pretty much all the preparation. When I show up, I'm not educating. I'm consulting. Big difference."

"How much time did you spend on that showing between the prep, the showing itself, everything?"

"Today? Those thirty minutes. The system spent about two hours on the packet and pre-qualification beforehand. But that wasn't my two hours."

Wade didn't respond. He was thinking about his own showings. The frantic twenty minutes before each one, pulling comps on his phone in the car. The clients who arrived having seen the listing online and nothing else, always full of questions he should have anticipated. Three hours per showing when you counted the drive, the prep, the follow-up he always meant to do and sometimes did. Multiply that by two or three showings a week and the math was staggering. Not for what it cost, but for what it did not produce.

Just as he was checking the time before heading to his own showing, his phone buzzed. His clients. Something had come up, they didn't say what, and they'd reach out to reschedule. He stared at the screen.

"That happen a lot to you?" Wade asked, looking up at Terry.

"Not really," she said. "If it's on my schedule, it usually sticks. Speaking of which, lunch? It's on me."

At noon, Terry stopped and did nothing else. This undid him. She didn't scroll her phone while eating. She didn't take a call. Her laptop stayed closed. He didn't remember her opening it once after they'd left the office. They ate at a small café two blocks away, sat at a table by the window, each ordered a sandwich, and they talked.

"How many transactions did you close last year?" Wade asked.

"Thirty-five. I have a firm rule, Monday through Thursday only. Home by three-thirty most days. I could probably do more if I wanted to."

"Do you mind me asking the revenue?"

"About three-eighty. Give or take." She set down her sandwich. "I took home around two hundred from those transactions. Tax man takes his cut. But I have a couple of other lines that add to that. Net was about half a million last year."

Wade set his own sandwich down. He knew agents who made that much, but they were strung so tight he'd made it a point to never want that life. He mumbled under his breath about Sloan and how she was always working. She sold more than Terry, but she looked so much more worn by it. Terry looked fresh and relaxed.

Terry heard his comment. "I know Sloan well. We've known each other a long time." She said it without judgment, the way you'd report a measurement. "I know what it costs her. That's a hard way to live."

She moved on before he could follow the thread. He let it go.

"So how do you..." Wade trailed off. The question he wanted to ask was too big. It contained every other question. His father's journals, his own messy thoughts in journals he kept, Peyton's sentence, the three years of checking boxes that produced nothing. It all collapsed into something he couldn't find the word for.

Terry waited.

"I made a commitment to myself and my family a long time ago to only do what was necessary and sufficient for my business," she said. "I have systems to handle a lot, but that's not where it begins. I need those systems to implement a vision. The vision comes from experience, learning, and thinking."

"I don't know that I have time for all that right now," Wade said. He heard the edge in his own voice and regretted it immediately. She'd invited him to spend the morning with her. She'd bought him lunch when his client cancelled. She didn't deserve that tone.

She smiled. Not the practiced kind, but the smile of someone who'd just found what she was looking for. "Tell me then, Wade. What are you stuck on?" She took a sip of her iced tea. "Think about what you watched this morning. Everything I did took time I'd made sure I had. Why do you think that was?"

She let it sit. He didn't respond. Waited for her to explain it.

"My actual work today was about an hour and a half of being fully present with people who matter. Everything that made that hour and a half effective happened before I sat down. Not because I worked more hours. Not even because of the technology. Because I knew my goal, and I knew the constraint."

"What's yours?" he asked.

"Let's not make this about me," she said. "I'll tell you more about how I got here another time. What are you stuck on?"

He didn't want to let it go. "Don't your clients expect more access? More availability? Sloan says that's what sep—"

Terry cut him off. "My clients get more of me than they'd get from Sloan." She set down her glass. "When they're with me, I'm fully present. Not checking my phone. Not thinking about the next showing. I'm with them, completely. And they feel it." She paused. "But your clients aren't with me. Your clients need to be with you. So, what has you stuck?"

Wade sat with it. He'd been seeing a pattern in fragments for weeks, but it was like a single color jigsaw that he couldn't begin piecing together. He had the edge pieces, but those were simple. He knew the puzzle could be completed. He couldn't put it together.

"Wade." She leaned in slightly. "At some point, we're all where you are right now. There isn't an answer yet, I don't expect one. We'll find it. I just need you to keep thinking before we talk next time."

"Next time?"

"Yes, next time. But don't call me until you think you have the answer." She stood. "Come on, let's head back so you can get home."

Home. An oddly specific word. Like a direction, not just a destination.

He drove home on autopilot, the route so familiar his body handled it while his mind went elsewhere.

Everything he'd seen that morning contradicted everything he'd been told. Every meeting, every training, every mentor, every podcast. They all said the same thing in different packaging: do more. Make more calls. Hold more open houses. Be more available. Work more hours. Effort in, results out. The only variable was volume.

Terry worked less than anyone he knew. He was confident she made more than anyone in his office. And she seemed content. Which felt almost offensive in its impossibility. Not the manic, caffeine-fueled, closing-day euphoria that Wade had learned to mistake for the real thing. The quiet kind. The kind that comes from knowing where you're going and not being in a panic about getting there.

He compared that to Sloan. A lot of transactions, a lot of money, and, from what she'd let slip in unguarded moments, on her third marriage. He never saw her eat anything but protein bars, her phone buzzing like a trapped insect. He thought about the exhaustion she wore on her face. He thought about the way she'd said "That's what it takes" with the conviction of someone defending a choice she couldn't afford to question.

Terry wasn't doing more. She was doing different.

He pulled into his driveway. The windows were open. Through the kitchen window he could see movement. Peyton was home. He hadn't remembered her mentioning it. The girls were occupied somewhere inside while she read, decompressing from the week. He sat in the car for a moment and noticed that the knot behind his sternum felt different. It wasn't gone. But it had loosened like a fist unclenching one finger at a time.

He went inside. Peyton looked up when he came through the door and her expression did something subtle. Not surprise exactly, but a small recalibration. She'd been expecting him much later. He'd walked in looking at her instead of his phone.

"Hey. You're home early."

"I am."

"How'd the showing go?"

He set his keys on the counter. Kelli was on the living room floor with crayons, working on something with the ferocious concentration she brought to all artistic endeavors. Amelia was at the kitchen table with a chapter book, legs tucked under her in a position that looked uncomfortable and apparently wasn't.

"I don't know yet," Wade said. "I saw something today I'm still trying to make sense of."

Peyton really looked at him. The way she used to, before looking had been replaced by the quick assessment of which version of Wade had come home. She saw something she wasn't expecting. "Did the showing not go well?"

"It got cancelled. I ended up spending the morning with that Terry woman I mentioned. She works differently than anyone I've seen. I'm not sure what to do with it yet."

Peyton didn't say anything right away. Wade braced for what he probably deserved. The skepticism she'd earned through the last CRM, the lead generation service, the coaching program he'd almost signed up for. She'd watched him chase solutions the way she watched patients' families chase miracle cures. She had compassion for the hope. She was running low on it.

But what she said was: "Tell me about it."

Not how much does it cost. Not is this another thing you'll try for a week. Just: tell me about it. An open door.

So he did. He told her about the briefing that was ready before Terry arrived. The nine minutes and three video messages. The seller call where Terry told a client to wait. The showing where the buyers came in already prepared. The lunch where Terry closed her laptop and didn't check her phone once.

"She kind of sounds like your dad," Peyton said when he finished.

Wade blinked. He'd been thinking the same thing. Peyton saw it without being told because Peyton saw most things without being told. The fact that she'd said it out loud meant she was paying attention.

"Yeah," he said. "She does."

Kelli appeared in the kitchen doorway, holding a drawing with both hands, crayon still in her fist. "Daddy, look."

He crouched down. The drawing was a house. The kind a five-year-old draws, triangle roof, sun in the corner, smoke coming from a chimney they didn't have. In front of the house, four figures. Two tall, two small. All of them holding hands. All of them together.

"That's us," Kelli said. "That's our house, Daddy."

Wade looked at the drawing. He looked at his daughter's face, open and completely unguarded. Then he gave her a hug, exaggerated, shaking, the universal signal that he was about to squeeze her until she burst.

She squealed and ran back to the living room. Wade stood up. Peyton watched him, and in her expression he saw something he hadn't seen in months. Not hope. Peyton didn't trade in hope the way he did. Something more grounded than that. Cautious, but real.

He didn't promise her anything. He didn't say this is going to be different or I've figured it out. He just stood in his kitchen with his family around him and the memory of Terry's morning turning over in his mind. He felt the question deepen.

Not answer. Deepen.

What is my constraint?

He still didn't know. But for the first time, he knew what it looked like when someone had found theirs.

He didn't call Terry the next morning. Or the day after that. He needed room to think about it.

For the first time in three years, Wade gave himself some.

MORE OF THE SAME

The energy lasted until Monday.

Wade drove to the office that morning with a sense of direction. Not a plan exactly. Nothing that specific. More like the feeling you get when you've been walking in circles and someone shows you a path that leads to anywhere else. He'd spent the weekend turning Terry's morning over in his mind. The precision and purpose of all of it, the absence of waste lodged a feeling in him the same way his father's journals did. He had evidence that a different way existed.

What is my constraint?

Over the weekend, the weight of finding the right answer shifted. It felt lighter. He didn't know the answer, but he had some hope. Terry's business showed him it was possible. His father's journals showed him what it looked like. He just needed to find it.

Wade parked in front of the Turner office, gathered his things, and exhaled a deep, calming breath. He walked in. Sam was standing at the front of the bullpen, which was never a good sign on a Monday morning. Sam at the front of the room meant an announcement. Sam's announcements were seismic proclamations. They formed suddenly and moved fast. Wade always thought that Sam intended them to be earth shattering.

"Perfect timing, Wade. Grab a seat. Big things."

Wade grabbed a seat in the half-full conference room. About a dozen agents sat in the room. Sloan waited, planner open, pen moving. Jordan was missing, which Wade assumed that meant Jordan would arrive in ten minutes looking like he'd been somewhere more important.

"Okay, team." Sam clapped his hands. "Social media. I know, I know — we've talked about it. But I was on a call Friday with a marketing company, and here's what they told me that blew my mind." He turned to the whiteboard and wrote "DAILY CONTENT" in block letters, underlined. "Daily. Not three times a week. Not when you feel like it. Every. Single. Day. The biggest names in content production are talking about it. I think we need to take that advice to heart."

He turned back to the room with the expression of a man who discovered fire. "They're going to track it. Engagement metrics; likes, comments, shares, saves. Weekly reports. They've got a dashboard. And here's the kicker—" Sam pointed at the room as if selecting each of them individually for something important. "The agents on their platform who post daily are seeing a forty-seven percent increase in lead generation."

Wade looked at the whiteboard. DAILY CONTENT. He thought about Terry's morning. The three-minute briefing. The nine minutes of video messages to specific people about specific things. The twelve-minute seller call. The thirty minute showing. The particular quality of Terry's attention where every minute focused on a person, a relationship, a conversation that mattered. None of it directed at an algorithm.

"Now, I know what some of you are thinking," Sam said, apparently reading a room that was thinking nothing at all. "'Sam, I don't have time for daily posts.' And here's what I'd say to that. You don't have time not to. This is where the eyeballs are. This is where the leads are going to come from. If you're not showing up every day, someone else is showing up every day, and that someone else is getting the client you should have gotten."

The logic was tight, but it was circular. Self-reinforcing logic rarely has a flaw when you initially look. This was Sam's way of thinking, though. Wade wrote "daily content, engagement metrics" in his journal. Writing things down was what he did when he didn't know what else to do. Then he sat through the remaining twenty minutes of the meeting feeling the energy he'd carried into the parking lot drain through the floor like water through a cracked foundation. Wade felt deflated after leaving the conference room.

Jordan caught him in the hallway afterward, materializing beside him mid-stride, coffee in hand, already in the middle of a conversation Wade didn't know he was having.

"Wade. How's the week shaping up?"

"Working on it. Following up on a couple leads," Wade replied. He hid his annoyance at the question, though.

"Very nice." Jordan nodded. The same nod as always. His tone was unenthusiastic. "I've got nine confirmed. Plus two listing appointments. It's going to be a good week." Factual and direct, consistent with Jordan's style. Wade always felt like he was supposed to see Jordan's numbers as no big deal. "You hit any of those networking events last week?"

"Didn't have time."

"Make time, brother. That's where the relationships are." Jordan clapped him on the shoulder. Always the shoulder. Always the clap. The physical punctuation mark that said I'm helping you and

I'm better than you in the same gesture. And like that he was gone, already on his phone and somewhere else.

Wade stood in the hallway and thought about the word relationships. Jordan used it the way Sam used activity. A container for something that sounded right. When you opened it, though, nothing was there. Terry had relationships. Diane the seller, whose mother had died, was a relationship Terry seemed to value a lot. When her buyers arrived, she paid complete attention to their time together. The mortgage broker she'd thanked by name. What Jordan meant was contacts. Names in a database, handshakes at events, the accumulation of faces you recognized but didn't know.

The distinction was important, and at that moment Wade started to understand why. He felt — insulted — by the way Jordan talked to him. He knew Jordan didn't really intend it that way, but he hated it. Wade was a contact for him, a momentary exchange of words. Then, he had a brief thought that maybe Peyton felt the same way about him. It deflated him further.

Sloan found him at his desk. She had a particular radar for finding a moment when she didn't believe you were doing anything important. He was just thinking about the morning, his wife, Terry, and his Dad's journals. He was trying to connect pieces in his thinking, and he felt like Sloan might tell him he's procrastinating.

"Hey." She sat on the edge of his desk and looked at him with the warm concern of someone about to give advice you didn't ask for. "I heard you spent some time with Terry last week."

Wade felt a small jolt. This industry was a terrarium. Nothing happened without everyone eventually knowing. Wade didn't even really know how Sloan would have heard about it. "Yeah. She invited me to see how she runs her morning."

Sloan nodded slowly. "Terry's a good agent. Smart. Nobody's questioning that." She paused. The pause was loaded. "But she runs a very different kind of business, Wade. It's solid, but it's not what I'd call volume."

"She seems to do pre—"

"I know what she does." Sloan said cutting him off. "And her numbers are good. But her model doesn't scale. She works alone, she turns away a lot of business. She caps her own growth by design. That works for some people. But once you're doing real volume—" She swept her hand to indicate the office, the profession, the implicit universe of ambition she inhabited. "You can't systematize relationships. You can't automate trust. You have to be there. In the room. On the phone. Available. That's what clients need."

Wade stared at Sloan but didn't say anything. He just saw her in the moment. She looked so beaten and exhausted. He noticed her wedding ring was off. His thoughts immediately went back to Peyton and how devastated he'd be if he wasn't wearing his. She did a lot of work. He saw the toll it was taking.

"Look, I'm not saying Terry's wrong," Sloan said. "I'm saying there's a cost to going that route. You slow down, you lose momentum. You start turning away business, other agents pick it up. This industry doesn't wait for you." She slid off his desk. "Don't overthink it."

She left. Wade stared at his monitor feeling discomfort at trying to reconcile two truths that couldn't both be right. They pressed against each other in his chest. Sloan spoke from experience that dwarfed his. He didn't dismiss it. But everything he'd seen at Terry's contradicted what Sloan was saying. All Wade wanted was to go back to the feeling he had walking into the office that morning. Optimism. Hope. He even thought he was enjoying himself.

He tried so hard.

That was the thing he wanted credit for later, when the week collapsed around him. He tried. He sat at his desk Tuesday afternoon with notes and his phone. Just one thing from Terry's morning that he could implement was his goal. He took what he considered the most advanced CRM he had and got to work building a system for knowing who to contact and when and what to say.

Three hours later, the legal pad was covered with arrows and boxes, crossed-out names, and a diagram that resembled a flatfoot's conspiracy theory connected by red string. He'd started by listing his active leads. Forty-seven names. He couldn't remember most of them. He tried to categorize them: hot, warm, cold. The categories blurred because he didn't have enough information about most of them to know where they stood. He tried to build a contact schedule, but it fell apart when he realized he didn't know what he'd say to any of them. He hadn't maintained the relationships between contacts, and calling them now felt like showing up at someone's door after months of silence and pretending you'd just been in the neighborhood.

The diagram stared back at him. All arrows. No system.

Sam walked by. He glanced at the mess in Wade's work area and said, "Stop overthinking it, Wade. Just call them."

Wade cursed and threw his pen down in frustration.

Wednesday night, Peyton found him at 11 PM.

He was at the dining room table that served as his home office. His screen glowed in the dark house. He'd put the girls to bed an hour ago. Peyton had been on an odd shift and came home to find the kitchen cleaned and the girls asleep. She recognized Wade's look when she walked in. She'd seen this particular configuration of guilt and determination before.

She stood in the doorway. Still in scrubs. Hair pulled back.

"What are you working on?"

"Business systems." He said it with the slight defensiveness of a man who knows how it sounds. "Follow-up processes. Lead management. I'm trying to figure out how to organize—"

"At eleven o'clock at night."

"I couldn't sleep."

Peyton pulled out the chair across from him and sat down. She didn't look at the screen. She looked at him. Not unkindly. It was familiarity. She'd been in that dining room before and saw Wade in front of different screens, watching different versions of the same search.

"Is this going to be another thing you try for a week and then abandon?"

The sentence landed in his sternum. It wasn't cruel. Peyton wasn't cruel. It was accurate. She'd watched him cycle through fixes for three years. The lead generation service that was going to change everything. The coaching program he joined. The CRMs he'd paid for and never fully set up. The marketing strategy from the podcast that lasted eleven days. Each one arrived with the same energy he was sitting in right now. His late-night conviction that he'd found an answer never quite worked. Yet each one faded into the same pile of abandoned attempts.

"I don't think this is more of the same," he said.

"You've said that before."

He had. He knew he had. The words felt thin even as he said them, stretched over the same frame as every previous promise.

But something felt different about this. The journals, Terry's morning, the questions that wouldn't leave him alone. He couldn't prove it and she had no reason to believe it, but this felt different. Peyton stood up to leave him alone.

"I know you have to put up with a lot from me," he said as she started to walk away. "I just have a feeling it's different because I'm looking for something specific. I just don't know exactly what I'm looking for." Peyton smiled and lightly blew him a kiss before leaving.

Thursday, Wade came home early.

He told himself he'd keep doing everything he was already doing — the calls, the showings, the open houses, the daily social media Sam was now pushing for. Plus he'd add Terry's ideas on top. More, not different. Layer the new onto the old. He could handle both. Eventually the new methods would replace the old and he'd find what he was looking for.

That same afternoon, another showing canceled. For one accidental evening, there was nothing pulling him away from home. By 5:30, Peyton was cooking dinner. Amelia read at the kitchen table, legs tucked beneath her in the pretzel position she favored, her chapter book held close like a secret. When she looked up at Wade working at the table, she had the same expression she always had when he was around — happy he was there, but not expecting him to be.

"Hi, Daddy."

"Hey, sweetheart."

She returned to her book.

Kelli was at the other end of the table, surrounded by a debris field of crayons and paper. Deep in conversation with herself:

total, ferocious, impervious to distraction. She had a purpose, and that purpose was to create.

Eventually, Wade asked her, "What are you drawing, Kel?"

She held it up.

It was a kitchen scene. Their kitchen. The table he was sitting at, drawn from above the way kids draw rooms when they're trying to fit everything in. Four place settings. A pot in the middle with steam coming off in three squiggly lines. Four figures around the table, all sitting, all eating. Kelli had drawn herself with a fork halfway to her mouth. Amelia had her book open beside her plate, which Kelli had clearly noticed and reproduced with the care of a five-year-old documenting the truth. Peyton stood at the stove in the corner of the page, ladle in hand. Wade was at the head of the table.

He was not on his phone. He was looking at Peyton. He had the small smile he made when he was actually paying attention. His hands weren't holding anything.

In the corner of the page, in handwriting Wade hadn't realized she could do yet, she'd written DINER NIGHT.

"That's tonight," Kelli said.

"That's tonight," Wade repeated.

"And tomorrow," Kelli said. She picked up a yellow crayon and added another sun in the upper corner, next to the one already there. "And the day after."

She wasn't looking at him. She was finishing the picture. The two suns sat side by side in her sky, evidence of days she had already drawn into her version of the world.

"Can we put it on the fridge?"

He tore off a piece of tape from the dispenser Peyton kept near the phone. He pressed the drawing onto the fridge between a grocery list and a magnet from Amelia's school. He smoothed the edges and sat back down at the table.

The two suns were the part he kept looking at.

Tonight he'd come home by accident. He'd been planning to layer the new onto the old. More, not different.

The drawing was already a step ahead of him.

Peyton watched from the counter. She'd seen the drawing. She didn't say anything. She didn't need to.

Wade stood in front of the refrigerator and looked at his daughter's picture. He felt something settle into him that was different from guilt. Different from shame. Even different from the late-night resolve that burned hot and faded by morning. It was quieter than any of those.

He didn't change that night. He didn't call Terry. He didn't tear up the compromise he'd made at the dining room table or throw away the diagrams or do anything that looked, from the outside, like transformation. He ate dinner with his family and helped Kelli with her bath. Before bed he read Amelia a chapter of her book. And he kissed Peyton goodnight before lying in the dark thinking about the drawing. He was smiling in the picture, so he needed to find out how to do it in real life.

The drawing was there when he poured his coffee the next morning. It was there Saturday afternoon when he left for an open house. It watched him from the kitchen with the silent patience of the truth. It didn't argue, insist, or raise its voice. It just stayed there, waiting for him to look.

Wade wasn't ready to look again. Not yet. But the drawing was patient. Every morning when he poured his coffee he saw it. The family dinner showing happiness and togetherness. And he couldn't stop seeing it. He couldn't stop wanting it to be real.

He felt he had found what he was looking for, even if he didn't completely know what it meant.

Crisis Point

The call came on a Tuesday.

Wade was in his car between showings. They produced nothing but a follow-up call he dreaded. His phone rang from a number he didn't recognize. Most of these calls were spammers selling something to agents they didn't need or tire-kickers asking about a listing without identifying themselves. The area code was local, though, and Wade had a feeling this might be a call worth answering.

"Hello. This is Wade," he answered.

"Mr. Roberts? My name is Esteban Gabaldon."

The name hit him in the chest before his brain caught up. Gabaldon. The composition notebooks on the shelf above his father's workbench. The careful handwriting. Brought tamales from his mother's recipe for the shop. Sent seven of his people to us the next week. Good man.

"I knew your father," Esteban said. His voice had a quality Wade hadn't heard much in business calls. He was unhurried, the cadence of someone who had decided long ago that important things deserved their full measure of time. "Jon and I worked together for fifteen years. He was a man I respected enormously."

"Yes, sir. I... thank you. I found his journals recently. Your name is in them."

A pause, but not an empty one. The kind that holds something. "Ah yes, those old journals," Esteban chuckled as he responded.

"I just found them recently. I didn't know he wrote so much about every customer. What was going on in their lives. What mattered to them." Wade realized he was talking about it without having rehearsed any of this in the parking lot. It came out instinctually. "One of the entries mentioned tamales."

Another warm chuckle on the phone from Esteban. Something that held fifteen years of Tuesday mornings at a mechanic's shop where a man remembered your mother's recipe. "He was a good man, your father. The best I knew in business. He understood that the car was just the reason people walked in the door."

Wade gripped his phone tighter. His mother's words. Almost exactly.

"I'm calling because I have a need," Esteban said. "I'm looking for an estate property west of Atlanta. Fifteen acres or more, private, within thirty-five minutes of the airport. Spanish colonial architecture. Something authentic, not the suburban builds we see. I'm happy to renovate, but the bones must be right. My budget is three point eight million." He said the number directly and without emphasis.

Wade's mouth went dry. At a standard split, that was more than twice what he'd grossed last year. More than he'd earned in any single year of his career.

"I've been interviewing agents," Esteban continued. "Haven't found the right one yet. I spoke with your mother recently. She mentioned you are an agent now, and I thought if your father was that good, you might be too. I also called Jordan Whitfield, whose family represented clients in my circle for some time. I'd like presentations from both of you in two weeks. I want to see how you think about my situation."

"Mr. Gabaldon... yes. Absolutely. I'd be honored."

"Esteban." A quiet chuckle, then another pause. "Your father called me Esteban."

They hung up. Wade sat in the parking lot with the phone in his lap and his hands shaking. He had the vertigo of a man who has just been handed the thing he's been praying for and realizes he doesn't know what to do with it.

A few days later, Wade was throwing everything at it. After Gabaldon's assistant had emailed details that matched what Esteban said on the phone, Wade started pouring everything he had into it. On top of the showings and the daily content Sam now tracked on a dashboard, Wade carved the time from sleep and from the thin margins that weren't already claimed. Peyton understood, at least. He'd shown her the journal entries, told her where Esteban's name came from. She'd given him room to be consumed, and he took all of it.

He researched the market west of Atlanta with thoroughness that bordered on mania. Every listing within thirty-five minutes of Hartsfield-Jackson above two million. Historical sales data. Tax records. Zoning regulations. He pulled comps on properties sold in the past eighteen months. He built spreadsheets tracking price per acre, architectural style, lot dimensions, and proximity to the airport. He created a presentation deck with aerial photographs and market trend lines. Thirty-six slides, a cover page that read "Gabaldon Property Acquisition: A Comprehensive Market Analysis."

He tried to use what he'd learned from Terry. He'd watched her spend nine minutes on three video messages, each one personal, each one directed at a specific person about a specific thing. So Wade recorded a video for Esteban. It was seventeen minutes long and covered the entire Atlanta luxury market with the scattershot energy of someone trying to prove how much he knew.

He'd watched Terry prepare a buyer packet that anticipated questions before they were asked. So Wade prepared a packet. Forty pages of data, graphs, market analyses, neighborhood profiles anticipating every possible question without understanding which questions Esteban would actually ask.

He was using Terry's tools the way you'd use a scalpel to chop wood. The form was there. The thinking behind it was missing.

The rest of his business deteriorated. Follow-up calls weren't made. Two showing appointments fell through because he'd been too distracted to confirm them. The daily content requirement became a source of low-grade panic. He posted recycled market statistics at 11 PM. Peyton moved around him and through the house like someone navigating furniture in the dark.

He didn't notice. He had to impress Esteban Gabaldon. The preparation consumed him so completely that the distinction between working hard and working well had dissolved into the familiar blur of more. More slides. More data. More hours. The old approach wearing the new approach's clothes.

The night before the presentation, his laptop crashed.

The screen went black with no warning. He had worked since eight, building the final version of the deck, when the machine seized. He sat in the dark dining room. Peyton and the girls were completely asleep. The house was quiet since Wade had learned a long time ago to work quietly so he didn't interrupt his family. He pressed the power button and waited.

It came back on, but it didn't come back on the same. The file was corrupted. Three days of presentation work gone. His presentation, now forty-eight slides with custom graphics, market analysis, and clear recommendations he'd painstakingly formatted, was gone. He had an earlier version saved, but sections were missing. Formatting was off in others. He'd dropped a stack of papers in a windstorm and recovered what he could.

Wade rebuilt it until 3 AM. Stitched together what he could. Fixed what he could fix. Left what he couldn't and told himself it was good enough. He slept but not well. The residue of adrenaline mixing with the physical exhaustion of a man who ran a marathon he hadn't trained for. The face in the bathroom mirror didn't looked recovered from the work. He just looked pained by it.

Esteban's office was in a converted warehouse near the Westside Provisions District. High ceilings, exposed brick, the kind of space that announced taste without flaunting it. Wade arrived twelve minutes early with his laptop and his rebuilt deck. He didn't have any energy for this, but he did his best to fuel with caffeine.

Esteban waited. He sat behind a simple walnut desk: dark wood and uncluttered. Photos of his family adorned a wall. Floor to ceiling windows allowed in all the sunlight from the day, and outside was a small patio with plants, comfortable chairs, and a small table. He wore a gray sport coat and no tie. He stood when Wade entered and shook his hand. The grip was firm, but measured. Wade knew by the handshake this was Esteban's environment, but he was welcome to earn his place in it.

"Wade. Thank you for coming. Please." He gestured to the chair across from him.

Wade set up his laptop without saying a word. His hands were steady, which surprised him. Less than twelve hours earlier, his laptop had completely frozen. He wasn't entirely sure it would again. If it did, he wasn't sure how he'd pivot. While the computer booted, he handed Esteban the prepared packet of information that corresponded with the slides. He opened the reconstituted deck of forty-one slides. He didn't notice the slight tightening of Esteban's mouth as he watched him prepare.

"Mr. Gabaldon — Esteban — I've done extensive research on the market west of Atlanta, and I've identified ten properties that meet your criteria across multiple dimensions. I'd like to walk you through each one, along with the market data that supports each recommendation."

Wade presented thoroughly, competently, exhaustively. He covered the market trends. He showed the aerial views. He walked through the comps and the tax histories and the zoning considerations. He delivered every slide with every remark in forty-five minutes. As he closed, Wade felt triumphant. No sputtering, though. Esteban asked two questions, one about a specific property's water access, one about another property's proximity to new development. Wade answered both confidently and accurately.

Esteban's expression never changed, though. Wade realized the expression wasn't going to change, and his triumphant feeling turned to dread. Whatever Esteban was looking for wasn't in the slides. Wade didn't, in fact, have the answer to the questions Esteban wanted to really ask.

"Thank you, Wade," Esteban said when it was over. "Thorough work. I can see the effort." He stood and shook his hand and walked him toward the door.

He wasn't being unkind. Esteban did see the effort. Not the insights or the precision Wade put into it. He merely saw the effort. The praise you give someone who worked very hard at the wrong thing.

"Thank you, Mr. Gabaldon. May I ca—"

"Please, Esteban," he interrupted Wade. "My assistant will call you within a week or two. I'll make a decision soon about the direction I intend to go, but we will call you."

They shook hands again. Wade's hands were still steady. The rest of him wasn't.

Wade wondered what Jordan was presenting that afternoon. He knew that they both were meeting with Esteban that day. As he sat in his car in a Starbucks parking lot three miles away, he attempted to make phone calls but couldn't focus. Later in the day, he heard from Sam about the presentations. Jordan's presentation was polished, professional, the product of a team that knew how to effortlessly package information. Twelve slides. Three properties. A narrative about lifestyle delivered with the smooth confidence of a man who presented to wealthy clients since adolescence.

Ten days later, Wade heard from Esteban's assistant as promised. He'd chosen neither, but he did see some ideas he liked from both of them and wanted to see them again soon. The assistant didn't exactly know when, but he would reach out in due time when Esteban's calendar opened.

Wade hung up and sat with that sentence for a long time. He'd poured his heart and soul into getting that win. Although she understood the work it took, he couldn't help but feel like he'd let Peyton down and abused her patience. He felt like he owed it to Esteban to do better, but didn't know what that even meant.

He felt, beneath that, like he couldn't compare to his father. A mechanic who knew more about everyone than a real estate agent whose job was to work directly with people.

His father would have known. Jon, with his composition notebooks and his careful handwriting, would have heard the thing beneath the thing. The same way he heard that Deborah Simmons needed a safe tire more than she needed to save face. The way he heard that Bill Henderson needed permission to prioritize his daughter's graduation over a brake job. Jon would have listened, and the listening would have told him everything the market data couldn't.

Wade prepared to impress. And he failed.

Later that night was Amelia's dance recital.

She'd been preparing for a month. Wade watched her practicing in the living room: careful steps, counted beats, the seven-year-old seriousness she brought to anything she decided mattered. He watched her rehearse in front of the bathroom mirror, adjusting her arms, starting over when the timing wasn't right. He promised, three separate times, that he would be there.

He wasn't there.

He was reeling after the call from Esteban's assistant. Instead of going home he'd gone to the office, and at the office he'd opened his laptop and started reworking his approach for the second presentation. The reworking became research and the research became a spiral of calls and emails. His only response to failure was to work harder at the thing that created it. He called an agent about a listing that might match Esteban's criteria. He called another agent. After it became too late to call other people, he pulled up new comps. He started a new deck. He didn't look at the time.

When he did, it was 9:47 PM.

The recital started at seven. It was over by eight-thirty. He'd missed it entirely. And not just missed it, but he didn't realize it ended until an hour and seventeen minutes after his daughter had performed the routine she'd practiced for a month. The audience included her mother, grandparents, her sister, and an empty seat with a folded piece of paper on it that read "Daddy" in Amelia's careful handwriting. She wanted to make sure he could find her.

Wade didn't even care at what speed he drove home. The house was dark except for the kitchen light. He came through the door quietly, the way you enter a space where damage has already been done. Wade remained silent to remain hidden. The recital program sat on the counter. Amelia's name was circled in pencil. Beside it, the folded piece of paper. Daddy. The letters formed with the careful precision of a child who was learning cursive and using every new skill she had to write the word that mattered most.

Peyton was at the kitchen table. Not on her phone. Not reading. Sitting with her hands around a cup of tea that had gone cold, and an expression on her face Wade never saw before. It wasn't anger or disappointment. She was past the careful patience she'd maintained for three years. She wore the expression of someone who has arrived at a wall.

"The girls are asleep," she said.

"Peyton, I—"

"Amelia looked for you," she said quietly. "She looked for you three times during the performance. I watched her. She'd do a turn and her eyes would go to your seat. Every time." Her tone was matter-of-fact. Her body language, though, showed tension that Wade could feel across the room.

Wade stood in his kitchen with his keys in his hand and his briefcase on the floor. Behind him, the two drawings hung side by side on the refrigerator. Amelia's was the older one — the school portrait from Ms. Patterson's class, careful and dated, the family lined up in crayon. Peyton in scrubs. Amelia holding Kelli's hand. Wade off to the right, smaller than the others, holding a rectangle that was meant to be a phone.

Beside it, Kelli's: the kitchen scene, four around the table, two suns in the corner, Wade with his hands empty and his eyes on Peyton. *DINER NIGHT* in the corner.

The old picture was where he'd been. The new one was where Kelli had drawn him going. He was standing in the kitchen exactly between the two, and he had nothing for either. No defense. No explanation that didn't sound like every other explanation. No promise that didn't crumble under the weight of every previous promise.

"I can't do this anymore," Peyton said. She said it the way she said things at work with clarity and without excess. The sentence of a woman who spent three years asking for something and was now stating, with the finality of a medical assessment, what she observed. "I'm not going to ask you to choose. But I do expect it, Wade. If you have to make a choice, I hope you make the right one. I won't watch you destroy yourself, and us, in the process."

She got up. She put her cup in the sink. She went to bed.

Wade sat at the kitchen table. Motionless. Emotionless. Empty.

The house ticked around him. The refrigerator cycle, the furnace hummed, and small random sounds a house makes when nobody's talking were all he heard. He sat in the chair Peyton vacated, still warm. And he felt her sentence pressing against everything he'd been trying to build for three years. Right now it all seemed wasted. All the effort, wasted.

He got up and walked to the living room. He found some of his father's journals on the shelf where he'd last put them. These were beside the family photos and the books Peyton read on her days off. He already knew the page he was looking for. He'd read it enough times that his hands found it the way you find a light switch in a dark room.

Gabaldon, Esteban — fleet maintenance, quarterly. Brought tamales from his mother's recipe for the shop. Told me his man-ufacturing contacts are struggling. Recession hitting the suppliers hard. I mentioned we were slow too. He sent seven of his people to us the next week. Seven. Didn't ask for anything. Just said good mechanics are hard to find and he wanted to make sure we stayed open. Just a damn good man. I miss having him around.

Wade read the entry. Then he read it again. He closed the journal and sat with it in his lap. The weight of it settled over him, heavy and undeniable. The weight of a lesson he'd been staring at for months without learning.

His father had known Esteban. He didn't know how, but he really understood him. Jon Roberts knew this man through a simple, deliberate act of noticing what mattered, writing it down, and honoring it. Yes, Jon Roberts understood Esteban Gabaldon the way he'd understood every customer who walked through his shop. But there was something more Wade figured. Wade knew if he could figure out what made this entry so special that the man it mentioned called him specifically, he could win the work.

Wade prepared ten properties and never once asked what Esteban was looking for. His father would have known, and if he didn't he would have asked. More importantly, his father would have listened. He would have known, before a single property was mentioned, what this meant to the man.

The clock on the microwave read 11:24. Wade picked up his phone and called.

Terry answered on the second ring. Unhurried, even at this hour. As if a phone ringing late at night was simply something that had happened, and she had decided to respond to it.

"Terry. It's Wade."

"I know. Everything alright?"

"I need help." He heard himself say it, and for the first time in three years the sentence didn't come with qualifications. No I need a few tips. No I was wondering if you had a suggestion. No softening, no performance, no attempt to frame the asking as something smaller than it was. "Real help. I'm going to ruin everything in my family. I already am. Can you help?"

Then silence. The kind he remembered from the first phone call.

"Good," she said. "Come over tomorrow morning. Bring your complaints."

"My complaints?"

"Everything that isn't working. Everything that pisses you off. Everything you think you're ruining. Just bring it all."

Wade looked at the refrigerator. Both drawings in the light from the stove hood, the only light left on in the kitchen. Amelia's portrait of who he'd been. Kelli's *Diner Night* of who he could still be. He couldn't change the first one. But the second one was still possible.

"I'll be there," he said.

They hung up. He felt something he hadn't felt before. Not hope. He'd burned through hope and every replacement for it.

Something closer to surrender. He'd run out of ways to avoid the thing he needs to do.

He didn't feel better. He felt emptied. Scraped clean. Black and bare and, to anyone passing by, destroyed.

Wade turned off the stove hood light. He walked down the hall. He stopped at Amelia's door, open the way she liked it, and looked at his daughter sleeping in the glow of her nightlight. She was curled on her side, one arm around a stuffed rabbit, her face smooth in sleep.

He stood there for a long time. He wanted to wake her up and apologize. But he went to bed.

Tomorrow, he would bring his complaints. And for the first time in three years, he would start building something that actually worked for his family.

Getting Focused

He drove to Kennesaw the next morning with the windows down.

The weather didn't call for it. Fifty-three degrees and overcast, the March morning couldn't decide what it wanted to be. But, Wade needed to feel the rush of air. It moved across his face and his hands on the wheel and kept him in his body. His mind was somewhere else entirely. Still at the kitchen table. Still in the dark. Still holding the sentence Peyton had left behind like a stone in his pocket.

I can't do this anymore.

Wade passed the Turner & Associates exit and didn't take it. Just about every morning for three years, that exit had been the first turn of the day. This time he let it go. As a newer real estate agent, the Turner office was his gravitational pull. The density of social media dashboards, call logs, and activity always pulled him back. Just the act of passing felt like escape velocity. He knew he didn't need permission to be elsewhere, but it still felt liberating.

He'd slept four hours. He'd woken before the alarm, dressed in the dark, and stood in the kitchen pouring coffee while girls' drawings watched him from the refrigerator. So, he watched back. He wanted to carry the drawings with him as a reminder of what he needed to do. Instead, he wrote — not texted — a note explaining to Peyton why he left early and where he'd be. He took one last drink of coffee, and left the house.

Wade arrived at Terry's office and felt like the journey was really about to start. It was exactly as he'd left it the last time they met months ago. The small front area with the desk, the living plant, the framed photograph of the girl in the swimming cap. The morning he'd shadowed Terry, this had been an alien landscape. Then, it was odd in how calming and peaceful it was. Now he walked toward it knowing why he was here. Before he'd come as a visitor. Now, he felt like an explorer.

Terry was in the back kitchen area. Just like before, she came out with two coffee mugs when he arrived. Again: unhurried and waiting for him so they could get started. She handed him one and signaled for him to come sit in her small, but spacious, conference room. She didn't ask how he was doing. She didn't mention the late-night phone call or the desperation that had been in his voice when he'd made it. She just sat, and sipped, and waited.

"I don't know where to start," Wade said, breaking the silence.

"Yes, you do." Terry set her mug down. "I said to bring your complaints. So bring them."

"My complaints?"

"What pisses you off the most right now? Just talk."

He started slow and reserved. He didn't intend to overshare and put all of it on Terry.

As he talked, though, it was like a dam breaking. He couldn't hold it anymore. He talked about time. About how there was never enough of it, how sixty hours a week produced twenty hours of actual work and forty hours of what he was starting to suspect was elaborate avoidance. He talked about the fifty leads that cost him money and attention and produced, after the whole machine had chewed through them, maybe one or two closed transactions. He talked about the calls he made that no one answered and the calls he didn't make because he couldn't remember who the person was or what they'd talked about or why he'd written their name on a napkin at a networking event three months ago.

He talked about Sam's meetings and how much he hated them. The motivational noise. Dashboards measuring activity the way a pedometer measures steps. The focus on dutifully counting indifferent to where they led. He talked about every time Jordan clapped his shoulder and how guilty he felt when he wanted to punch him. He talked about Sloan's advice, but about how sad he felt for her. As of late, he increasingly worried if he'd end up divorced like her.

Then talked about the Gabaldon meeting. He was angry at himself for the hours lost and the work he poured his soul into. He was angry at Jordan that he was afforded the opportunity by his own family connections, and how badly he wanted to win this one. Wade surprised himself a bit when he admitted — out loud — that he resented Esteban's assistant calling him.

Finally, he started to talk about Amelia's recital, the drawings on the refrigerator, and his guilt. He held this in his soul every time he let Peyton down. He talked about Peyton's face in the kitchen light and the sentence she'd said and the way she'd gone to bed afterward without waiting for a response. And he shared how he had no response that meant anything, because he used up all the ones that did and she stopped believing them.

He stopped. He didn't run out of things to say. He ran out of air.

Terry had been writing, but not constantly. She looked at him through most of it, listening with the quality of attention he noticed with her clients. Wade felt like she was holding that space open just for him. Occasionally, she jotted things down on a yellow legal pad. Short phrases. Something more like surveying. Marking where the ground was solid and where it was soft.

She finished writing. She looked up.

"Good," she said. "Now we know where to start."

Wade let out something that was half breath and half laugh. "That's it? I dump three years of chaos on you and you say good?"

"No one's ever listened to the whole thing, have they? Have you even said all of that before?"

He started to answer and stopped. She was right. He complained before, but always in fragments and edits. He never shared his financial fears with Peyton. He was never honest with Sam about how he felt unmotivated. He never talked about his family with his colleagues because he assumed they didn't really need to know or care. No one had ever heard the entire thing at once, because he never said the entire thing at once. Sharing the full, unfiltered brain dump was a new experience.

"No," he said.

"That's part of why it persists. You can't fix what you can't see whole." Terry tore the page off the legal pad and set it between them on the table. "But we're not going to fix all of this. Not today or all at once. Some of these things may never be fixed. What we're going to do is find the one thing that matters most. Your constraint."

She got up and walked to the whiteboard on the wall behind her desk. She picked up a black marker and drew a horizontal arrow. Then she drew a shape around it. Open and wide on both ends, narrowing to a point in the middle.

"Your business," Terry said, tapping the pipe, "is like this. What you want is flow. That's what this arrow is. Flow through the pipe is what produces results. In your case, closed transactions.

Everything you do, every hour you spend, every lead you chase, you'd think it should automatically increase flow."

She drew more arrows feeding into the left side of the narrowing. "The point where the pipe gets narrow is the constraint. No matter how wide the lead-in is, you can only fit so much through the constraint. No matter how much effort you put into lead generation, marketing, showings... Flow can never exceed what the narrowest point allows." She tapped the constrained portion.

Wade looked at the drawing. Simple. Almost embarrassingly simple. A pipe with a bottleneck. He could have drawn it on a napkin. If it was this simple, why was he struggling so hard to find his answer? The visual was so obvious he felt embarrassed it had taken this long to see it.

"So what are you supposed to do? Make the pipe bigger?"

"Eventually, yes. But first we need to know what it is and make sure it gets your attention. So let's map yours. Not the business you wish you had. The one you actually have. Walk me through it. What happens when a lead enters your world?"

Wade stood up without deciding to. He took the marker Terry offered, went to the whiteboard, and started drawing. What came out was messy, but it was accurate.

"Lead comes in," he said, writing it. "And I have them from all over: the big real estate sites, social media, referrals, networking event, whatever. I get maybe fifty a month."

"That's pretty good," Terry said, and she meant it. "What happens then?"

"I try to contact them. Within twelve hours, usually. Hopefully sooner, sometimes not. Depends on what else is going on." He wrote it. "Of the fifty, I reach about forty."

"Then what happens?"

"I try to get them interested. Send them listings, answer questions. Of the forty I reach, maybe thirty express some kind of interest."

"And what do you do with those thirty?"

Wade paused. The marker hovered. He could feel the answer forming before he said it, but he didn't want to admit it. Until he mapped it on a whiteboard in front of another person, he'd never seen how it looked from the outside.

"I try to set an appointment. I say something like, 'Let's find a time to meet, I'd love to show you some options.' Maybe four or five say yes in some vague way."

"How many of those become actual appointments?"

"One. Maybe two, if I'm lucky. The others drift away. They stop responding, or they say they're busy, or we play phone tag for two weeks and it just dies."

"And of those two who actually sit down with you?"

"I usually get both to sit down. One every other month, roughly, actually signs an agreement."

Terry wrote his numbers on the board next to the pipe. She drew small tick marks at each stage. 50, 40, 30, 5, 2, .5. Then she drew a circle around the gap between 30 and 5.

"Look at your pipeline," she said. "Where does it narrow?"

Wade stared at the board. The numbers told a story he'd never read, because he'd never put them in a line before. Fifty leads became forty contacts became thirty interested became five vague yeses became two actual meetings became half a closing a month. The biggest drop was in the middle: thirty interested people, then five. Twenty-five people lost in a single step. Between *I'd love to* and any kind of real commitment, the floor fell out.

He'd spent three years believing his problem was the front of the pipe. Not enough leads. Not enough contacts. Not enough people entering the system. That was what Sam preached. Make more calls, it's a numbers game and Wade just did it. He never examined the assumption that if he poured more water into the top, more would come out the bottom. But the numbers were right there on the whiteboard, and they said something different. They said the top of his pipe was fine. Fifty leads a month was plenty. The problem wasn't input. It was the place in the middle where the pipe choked down to nothing.

"There," he said, pointing at the gap between 30 and 5. "Between interest and a real yes. That's where I lose them."

"Why do you think?"

"Because there's nothing in that space. I go straight from 'they're interested' to 'hey, we need to meet right now.' I can't tell..." He trailed off. He was close to something. "I can't tell which of them actually mean it. I just try to get the meeting. And the meetings I do get, half of them are with people who were never serious. They're just looking. Or they're not pre-approved. Or they want to see twenty houses before they even think about making a decision. And I take all of them, because I'm afraid that if I don't, I'll miss the one who would have been easy."

"It sounds like you spend your best hours on your worst leads."

The sentence landed like a hand on his shoulder. That was exactly what he did. He spent hours showing houses to people who weren't really going to do anything with him. Meanwhile, his time with his wife and girls was being eaten up and spit out. All because he couldn't tell the difference between a real opportunity and a polite one. He'd never built the mechanism to tell.

"So what's your constraint?"

He stared at the board for two or three minutes. They felt like hours. Finally, he stated in the form of a question, "Qualification?" He said it and stood frozen in front of the whiteboard with the marker in his hand. Looking back at Terry, she smiled and nodded.

Then he felt something he hadn't expected: relief. Three years of listing symptoms; not enough time, not enough leads, not enough money, not enough hours. Underneath all of it, a single, specific, nameable thing. Not everything. One thing.

"That's the first step," Terry said. She took the marker from him, motioned for him to sit down, and wrote on the board:

1) IDENTIFY the constraint.

"What you just did is what most people never do. They skip straight to 'I need more leads' or 'I need to work harder' because they've never looked at where flow actually stops. You just looked, and you found it."

She turned back to the board and wrote the second step.

2) EXPLOIT the constraint.

"This means use it to full capacity with what you already have. Right now, you're not running a qualification process at all. You're skipping it. Before you buy new tools, before you change your marketing, before you do anything else: build a real qualification step and run every lead through it."

She continued to the third.

3) SUBORDINATE everything else.

"Every other part of your business should support getting people through qualification successfully. Not bypass it. Not run parallel to it. Serve it." She underlined serve it twice. "If your marketing generates leads that can't be qualified, fix your marketing process. If your follow-up doesn't move people toward a qualification conversation, redesign your follow-up. Everything feeds the constraint."

Wade looked at her. "But how do we actually grow?"

"Good question, but it's a little early. Focus is important first. If you don't subordinate your processes to the constraint, you can't grow. Like I said, people rush to the growth without understanding why they're not growing. Most people assume that making any part of the system better automatically improves outcomes. It doesn't. In some cases, it makes them worse. Which leads us to the next step."

She turned back and wrote.

4) ELEVATE the constraint.

"Once it's running at full capacity, once you've squeezed everything you can out of it with what you have, then you expand it. This is where tools come in. Technology. Systems. Leverage. But you can't elevate what you haven't defined."

Terry paused and let the next sentence arrive with its weight. "That's the mistake you made with Esteban. You tried to elevate a constraint you hadn't identified. You threw tools and hours at a problem you hadn't named. And so the tools did what tools always do when they're aimed at the wrong thing. They produced effort without producing understanding. I'm going to guess you didn't ask him one real question, did you?"

Wade felt the Esteban failure rearrange itself. Every minute, every slide, every desperate hour spent widening parts of the pipe that weren't the bottleneck. He'd been pouring water into both ends and wondering why nothing came out the middle. And Terry was right. When he thought back to the meeting in Esteban's office, not once did he stop long enough to actually hear him.

"I never qualified Esteban. I just assumed that because he knew my father, he'd know what I was capable of," Wade said looking at the floor. Then, he paused, and looked right at Terry. "It's not about what I'm capable of, though. It's about him. What's he capable of trusting me to do."

"Exactly! Even an Esteban needs qualification," Terry said pointing the marker at Wade. She was animated in her excitement. He could see these types of breakthroughs are what she really loved.

She turned to the board one final time.

5) Rinse and REPEAT.

"Once you elevate the constraint, a new one will appear. That's not failure. That's how systems work. The constraint moves. The thinking never stops. Business improvement isn't a destination you arrive at. It's a way of being. So, you start back at step one."

She set the marker down, sat back in her chair, and looked at him.

Wade stood in front of the whiteboard and looked at the five steps. This, right in front of him, was what he'd been searching for. It wasn't a solution, but something more fundamental. A way of thinking about problems that didn't start with doing more and didn't end with trying harder. All of it was dependent on observing, thinking, understanding, and acting.

He was starting to see how his father had done this with his journals. The careful attention to what each customer actually needed was always his focus. The willingness to look at the specific person in front of him rather than applying a general approach to every situation. Jon identified constraints his whole career. He never read a business book in his life. He just did it by instinct rather than by name.

"This is what he did," Wade said quietly.

Terry looked at him.

"My dad. Not like this, not with the steps written down. But the way he ran his shop. He knew exactly where his bottleneck was. It was trust. The car was just the reason people walked in the door. Everything else in his business he built to protect that trust, and he never wavered from it. All those people were so different, and he kept track of it in his journals."

Terry nodded. "Some people arrive at this by thinking it through. Some people arrive at it by living it. Your father lived it. We all have to live it eventually. The question is whether you're willing to do the work to understand it well enough to live it on your own."

The rest of their time together that day, they talked back and forth about how all of the things he complained about could be connected back to that qualification process. Wade also shared about some of his father's journal entries, and he started talking about his wife and girls in ways that made him feel whole again. Eventually, Wade and Terry agreed on a pause point.

She gave him an assignment at the front door, the way a doctor gives instructions at the end of an appointment. Clear, direct, simple.

"Go home. Finish mapping your actual process. Not the one you wish you had. Map the one you have. For each step: what happens, how long it takes, how many people enter, how many advance, and what specifically causes them to drop off. Real numbers. Real observations. No aspiration." She looked at him. "We can't improve what we can't see clearly."

Wade stood in the doorway with his keys in his hand. But he walked out with direction for the first time in his short real estate career. It had weight, substance, and purpose behind it. He was exhausted, still running on four hours of sleep and the residue of the worst week of his career.

He drove home in the early afternoon. The drive felt shorter than the morning. He thought about the simple pipeline on the whiteboard. Terry had said nothing about easy, but, it was simple. The constraint was there. It always was. He just never stopped long enough to look at the right place.

He compared the day to what he read in his father's journals. Jon didn't call it a constraint. He hadn't called it anything. He just knew. People needed their car fixed, but they absolutely trusted him to do it right. He built everything around protecting that. His schedule, his notes, his time.

There was something deeper he realized, too. The real constraint his father always worked to protect wasn't the business at all. It was being Wade's father. He decided, come what may, that he'd be present. The notes, the journals, the deliberate shop management were him subordinating the business of running an automotive shop to the business of being a dad.

That thought alone made Wade tear up.

Wade pulled into his driveway at 3:40 PM. Through the window he could see Peyton at the counter. The girls would be in the living room or at the table. They'd be doing the things they did in the late-afternoon hours when the house was theirs and the day was starting to wind down.

He went inside. Peyton looked up with a quick assessment in her eyes. She read him for exhaustion or the manic energy that meant he found another fix. He didn't know what she saw today. He hoped it was something different, though. He felt different walking through the door.

"Hey," she said, a bit surprised. "I got out of the hospital early today. Just needed to. You're home early."

Wade didn't say a word. He didn't explain anything of what happened in Terry's office. He didn't pitch her on the Five Focusing Steps or describe the pipeline or tell her this time was going to be different. Instead, he walked right up to her and wrapped his arms around her. He kissed her on the forehead. He asked about her shift, then he just listened.

Hesitant at first, Peyton talked. Instinctively, she shared with her husband the day she had, juicy gossip about people he didn't know, and funny memes the nurses shared amongst themselves. She enjoyed it. Wade enjoyed it more than anything, too.

After dinner and as the girls got ready for bed, he started writing. Not another plan. Just his business as it actually was. Mapping everything out step by step. He tried to emulate what his father wrote in his notebooks. What happened. What didn't happen. Where people entered. Where they disappeared. What he told himself about why, and what, underneath the telling, was actually going on.

It was harder than he expected. The writing was easy. It was the seeing. Every line he put down revealed something he avoided. Sometimes, he didn't understand why a particular outcome happened. The leads he chased for weeks that never went anywhere. Showings, follow-up calls, emails, social media — everything Sam preached and he practiced that was resulting in his miserable business.

The pipeline, drawn in his own handwriting, looked different from the one on Terry's whiteboard. Messier, but it was definitely more personal. The bottleneck wasn't an abstraction anymore. It was Tuesday afternoons spent driving to appointments with people whose names he'd forget by Friday. It was his life, hour by hour, spent on things that felt like work and produced nothing.

After the girls were in bed, Peyton came with a glass of water and set it beside him. She glanced at the diagram but didn't ask. She didn't leave, either. She lingered just long enough to see the question marks, circles, arrows, and boxes. She put her hand on his shoulder for a moment. It was heavy, but calming and reassuring.

He kept writing and the house settled around him. The normal nighttime sounds of his house started.

Every single one comforted him.

Inherited Fears

His notes and diagrams were starting to tell a real story.

Wade focused for three days on what he was mapping. It wasn't the obsessive focus that he spent on Esteban's presentation. He spent three evenings at the kitchen table after the girls went to bed. Peyton moved around him during those evenings the way she moved around a patient whose vitals have positively shifted. Watchful and supportive, but not overbearing. She didn't ask questions except to make sure he was okay.

She'd brought him water when she thought he needed it, coffee when she knew he'd want it. The third night she'd sat across from him with a book and read while he wrote. The silence between them changed. They hadn't run out of things to say. They just wanted to be in each other's presence. Peyton saw his work had focus. She didn't want to take away from that focus, but she wanted to experience it.

The next time Wade drove to Terry's office, he kept the windows up. He didn't need the air. What he was carrying felt different from anything he'd brought to a meeting before. All he had was his shapes, arrows, and numbers. They were all true and reflected his current reality. He avoided rounding up to make himself feel better.

Terry's office was the same. He was starting to understand that the sameness was the point. Terry had built a space where nothing competed for attention because attention was the thing she valued most. He let himself in. She was at the conference room table with coffee already poured. Two mugs, the legal pad from their last session stacked neatly to one side, his complaint list folded on top.

"Morning," she said.

"Morning." He sat down. Set his notes on the table between them. "I mapped it. The whole thing. Three days, real numbers, no B.S."

"Slow down. Let's have some coffee first." She slid his cup across the table and picked up the pad. She read what he'd written the same deliberate way she did everything else. No rushing, not performing the reading for his benefit. Just absorbing. Wade watched her eyes move down the page. Occasionally she'd nod. Occasionally tilt her head. He felt vulnerability showing someone what his business actually looked like when he stopped pretending it was working.

She set the pad down.

"Tell me what you see," Terry said.

Wade pulled the pad back and looked at his own handwriting. The boxes, the arrows, the numbers he'd revised twice because the first version had been unconsciously generous and the second version still lied about the follow-up rates.

"The numbers I gave you last time were pretty accurate," he said. "But I couldn't map out my lead qualification process. Because it doesn't exist. Not at all. It's just the numbers game."

He'd said it in the last session, standing at the whiteboard with the marker in his hand. But saying it then had been discovery. The shock of seeing the gap for the first time. Saying it now, after three days of sitting with it, was something else. Confirmation.

The difference between glimpsing something in a flash of light and seeing it in daylight, steady and undeniable.

"I try really hard to force a meeting," he said. "No real conversation. No attempt to understand if they're ready, or serious, or if I'm even the right person for what they need. I just try to get the appointment. Because the appointment feels like progress."

"And why do you do that?"

It was a simple question. Wade assumed Terry already knew the answer. He didn't, and therefore she was trying to help him find it.

He wanted to say something about efficiency and about not wasting time. If he wasn't the agent who moved fast, he'd be replaced. He started to say all of that. The words sounded like Sam's office, though, during Monday morning meetings. He felt like he'd be regurgitating motivation posters in the break room that no one questioned. How could he? It's hard to argue with generalities.

"I think I'm afraid," Wade said. "I'm afraid that if I ask too many questions, they'll think I'm wasting their time. They'll go find another agent who'll just show them houses without making them feel like they're being interrogated." Just saying it out loud felt like a shift inside of him.

Terry nodded for Wade to keep going.

"Every lead might be that one. That deal that's big enough I can actually stop working so hard. If I put up any kind of barrier, I'm afraid I'll lose them. I want them to find what they're looking for and get it done. I'm afraid they'll take their business to Jordan, or to whoever makes it easiest to get started." He paused to process what he said. "So I skip the conversation and go straight to the appointment, and half the time the appointment is with someone who was never going to do anything. Then I've lost an afternoon and gained nothing."

"Where do you think that fear comes from?" Terry asked. Wade started to answer, but she signaled for him to slow down. "Think about it first. Slow down, then answer."

Wade wanted to say it came from the experience of losing people who went with other agents. But Terry's question wasn't about what had happened. It was about where the fear had started. When he really traced it, that's not where he landed. His mind began to circle the Monday morning meetings every week.

"Sam," he said. "Sam's meetings. The whole culture of the office. 'Get them in the door. Get the appointment. Don't overthink it.' And watching Jordan operate. Jordan doesn't qualify anyone either, but it doesn't matter because his family name does the qualifying for him. His leads come pre-sorted. Mine don't, but I act like they do. I just assumed asking good questions would push people away. I've been told constantly it's hustle and numbers."

Terry got up and walked to the whiteboard.

She drew a shape Wade hadn't seen before. Not a pipeline. A cloud shape in the center, with boxes arranged around it, connected by arrows. It looked like a weather system diagrammed by an engineer: organic in outline, precise in logic.

"This is called an Evaporating Cloud," Terry said. She wrote the words above the shape. "It's a tool for understanding why a constraint persists even when you know it's a problem and genuinely want to fix it."

She wrote in the first box: *Close a sufficient number of transactions.*

"Your goal. Mine too, if we're being honest." She drew an arrow down to the left. "To generate more closed transactions, you must talk to more people." Wade nodded. That made sense, and that was exactly how he operated. She wrote: *Secure more client appointments.* Then drew another arrow to a box where she wrote: *Increase the quantity of leads.*

"We'll come back to this. But to close more transactions, you also must consistently qualify your appointments. That's what you found mapping your pipeline." Terry drew another arrow from the goal, this time down to the right. She wrote: *Qualify better clients.* Like on the other side, she drew an arrow to a box where she wrote: *Increase the quality of leads.*

She turned to him. "When you look at this, what do you see?"

Wade studied the diagram. He kept coming back to the words quality and quantity. "I'm having trouble with quality versus quantity. I don't know how I could do both."

She drew both arrows down to a single box at the bottom, where the two paths collided. She wrote: *CONFLICT.*

"To get more leads, you must skip hard qualification. To get better leads, you must absolutely qualify them. You can't do both. You can't simultaneously make it effortless to get started and ensure that the people who start are worth your time. So you're stuck. You oscillate. Some weeks you take everyone and burn your hours on bad appointments. Other weeks you try to be more selective and feel the panic of watching leads walk away. Neither approach resolves anything, because the conflict itself is the problem."

Wade felt it in his chest. The whiplash between wanting to be selective and being terrified to turn anyone away. The constant sense of choosing between two bad options. No matter which direction he leaned, something important got sacrificed. He'd never seen the shape of his own paralysis before. Never seen the internal war mapped out like a circuit diagram with a short in it.

"That's exactly what I feel," he said.

"I know." Terry tapped the conflict box. "And here's what matters: the cloud doesn't resolve by working harder on either side. You can't outwork this conflict. To close more transactions you absolutely need more leads and better leads. Those are the necessary conditions. Making more calls doesn't fix it. Being more disciplined about your calendar doesn't fix it. The conflict persists because there's an assumption underneath it that you've never examined."

She drew a dotted line from the left side, the skip-qualification side, back up to the goal, and wrote next to it: Asking good questions will cost me clients.

"That's the assumption. It's what makes the left side feel necessary. If you believe, really believe, in your gut that strong qualification drives people away, then skipping it feels like the only rational choice. But you can't leave out a necessary condition."

Wade stared at it. The assumption made sense, but something nagged at him. "If I qualify my leads and reduce the number coming in, won't that break the process on the other side?"

Terry set down the marker and held up her hand. He'd found the thread she waited for him to pull.

"So where did that assumption come from?" she asked. "Not the fear of not having enough leads, the assumption underneath the fear. The belief that a real conversation with honest questions about readiness and fit will close your pipeline completely."

Wade thought about it. He couldn't answer. When he tried to find a specific instance of a qualified, serious buyer leaving because he'd asked too many questions, he couldn't locate one. The leads he'd lost left for other reasons: price, timing, or indifference he'd mistaken for interest. Sometimes, but very seldomly, potential clients genuinely preferred a different agent's style. But he couldn't name a single client who walked away because Wade tried to understand what they actually needed.

"It just is," he said. "I guess it's the environment in Sam's office? I hear it a lot at industry conferences I've gone to. Even podcasts say the same thing. Remove friction, make it easy, and don't make the client work for it. Jordan doesn't ask questions. Jordan rolls out the carpet and lets people walk in. And Jordan closes deals." He paused. "But Jordan's family built the carpet decades ago. His leads already know who he is. They're already qualified by the time they call him. He's not skipping qualification, he's outsourced it to his last name."

Terry was quiet. She let the observation sit.

"I've been modeling my approach on someone whose situation is nothing like mine. Sam celebrates Jordan's numbers without asking where they come from. Sloan works nonstop and everybody calls her successful without asking what success is costing her. The whole system runs on assumptions nobody is questioning, because questioning them would mean admitting the system might be broken."

"And the assumption about qualification?"

"I've never tested it," Wade said. "Not once. I assumed that asking real questions would drive people away because everyone around me assumed it. But I don't have a single piece of evidence that it's true. Which means if I qualify better, I probably don't need as many leads to begin with."

Terry picked the marker back up. She went to the dotted line, the assumption, and drew an X through it.

"When the problematic assumption breaks," she said, "the cloud evaporates. There is no conflict."

She pointed to the left side. "Asking good questions doesn't cost you clients. It attracts the right ones and repels the wrong ones. You absolutely need more leads, but you need the right ones. You can have the conversation and still get the appointment. The conflict disappears. Not because you worked harder. Because you questioned what was holding it in place."

Wade looked at the whiteboard. The cloud with its boxes and arrows, the X through the assumption, the space that opened up where the conflict had been. And he thought about Esteban. Wade's presentation was competent, from a real estate standpoint. It had accurate facts, figures, and good properties. Except, none of it was good information because it wasn't relevant to Esteban.

Esteban never saw what he was looking for because Wade never bothered to ask. Esteban wanted to be invited into the process, most likely. The property wasn't just an investment in a portfolio. There were better agents than Wade for that. It was an investment in something deeper. Wade now suspected Esteban's history with his father was what made him reach out — to see whether Wade could be a similar kind of agent.

Wade skipped the conversation because the same assumption that choked his pipeline also choked his most important opportunity. He was afraid that asking questions would make him look unprepared. He assumed Esteban would choose Jordan, who wouldn't ask questions, who would just polish the surface and make it smooth.

Jon Roberts never called his process qualification. He called it listening. Every entry in those journals was the record of a man who asked questions and wrote down the answers. A man who built his business around what he heard. Jon understood, without a whiteboard or a framework, that the questions were the point. His customers wanted to know their car would be fixed, yes. But there was an entire reason that made the car matter to them.

"He never skipped it," Wade said quietly. "My dad. He never skipped the qualifying conversation. He just didn't call it that. He called it paying attention."

Terry nodded. "Your father had that instinct. You're going to build it by design. Both are valid. Design means you can teach it. You can develop the same intuition your father had, and pass it on."

Wade felt the weight of that observation. Not in his head, where the frameworks lived. Somewhere lower. Somewhere that held the image of his father's handwriting in the composition note-book. He felt Esteban's voice on the phone saying I knew your father. He ached believing his father's legacy had been lost on him.

Terry gave him his assignment at the front door. "Build a qualifi-cation framework," she said. "Not a script. Not a checklist you run through robotically. A set of questions that help you understand whether a prospective client is ready, aligned, and worth your time. And, just as importantly, whether you're the right agent for what they need."

"What's the difference? Between a script and what you're de-scribing?"

"A script is something you do to someone. A genuine conversa-tion is something you do with them. A script extracts information. A conversation builds understanding. The client should walk away from a qualification conversation feeling like they've been seen and heard, even if the conclusion is that you're not the right fit." She paused. "This isn't a gatekeeping exercise. It's a genuine experience. The difference matters."

"Thank you," he said.

Terry waved it off as if he offered to pay for coffee when the coffee was the least important part of the morning. "Don't thank me yet. Build the framework. Come back when it's done."

Wade thought about the cloud the whole drive home. He wondered how long he'd been living inside it. He oscillated between both sides for years, working harder on each in turn, never questioning the assumption holding the whole conflict together. Three years of grinding without ever considering that a conflict existed. Three years of believing the fear was a fact. Three years of building his business around an assumption he inherited from people who'd never tested it either.

The assumption wasn't even his. It came from Sam's meetings and Jordan's example. Wade wanted to be fair to them, it wasn't entirely their fault — the general ethos of the industry confused speed with service. Volume with value. These assumptions became the water everyone swam in. It had settled into him the way cold settles into a house through cracks around the window panes. He just forgot there was a different way to be warm.

The assumption broke. He could feel it as he pulled into the driveway earlier than any day in recent memory. He noticed, as he did more often lately, that his first look when he came home was for Peyton in the window. There she stood. At the counter in her same scrubs. He sat in the car for a moment, just noticing the ordinary thing of a house with people in it who were waiting, without waiting, for him to come through the door.

He went inside. Kelli hit him at knee level. He picked her up and she wrapped her arms around his neck and shook with the full-body commitment of her hug. Amelia looked up from the table where she was drawing and said, "Hey, Dad." She was still careful about which version was coming home. The missed dance recital was something that she wouldn't easily forget.

He carried Kelli to the kitchen table and set down his bag. He looked right at Amelia and asked, "Can I sit with you?" She smiled and nodded. He opened his bag and pulled out a notepad with all the work he'd been focusing on lately.

"What are we drawing, Daddy?" Kelli asked.

"I'm working on some questions. You know how you always ask me why?" He tickled her. "Well, I need to start asking why too."

She laughed, squirmed out of his grip, and ran off. What questions did he skip? What conversations did he avoid? He'd never once stopped to investigate the space between interested and appointment where people disappeared every month. Never asked why, never tried to understand what was actually happening there.

He had trouble thinking about clients at the moment, though. If he was honest with himself, he was worried about what his daughter thought of him. He let her down, and he needed to let her know that he wasn't okay with that. So, he put his pen down and looked at his older daughter again.

"Amelia? Can I ask you a question?" She looked at him and shook her head yes. She was confused, though, as if she expected to be in trouble for something. "Were you mad at me when I missed your dance?"

Amelia peered directly at him but didn't answer. It wasn't an answer. It was hurt, and she didn't really want to recall the night. She answered, "No. I'm just sad."

Wade felt it. The way she said sad made him feel like she believed it was her fault for him not showing up. It broke his heart that he caused that feeling in his daughter, but this was his first chance to learn what that meant. He didn't want to try and fix something that he didn't fully understand.

"Why did it make you so sad?" Wade asked. He invited Amelia to sit on his lap before she answered the question. For fifteen minutes, he just asked his daughter questions about why she felt the way she did. After each answer, he practiced telling her what he heard and asking if that's what she meant and why. Eventually, he learned that she was afraid he didn't like her dancing and that she was disappointed in herself for not being good enough.

Wade looked at his daughter directly in the eyes and said "Your dancing is beautiful. Sometimes, your dad just doesn't pay enough attention to that, and that's because he's afraid of not being good enough, too. Will you forgive me for missing the dance?"

Amelia, with tears in her eyes, hugged Wade tight and just said "You're a good dad." Then, she left his lap, grabbed her things, and went out to the living room to continue her drawing. Peyton, who had watched the entire exchange, brought him a glass of ice water.

"Can I ask you why you put up with me?" Wade said.

"I love that you're a dreamer," Peyton said. "I'm a realist. You need me, and I need you." She kissed his cheek and started to walk out of the kitchen.

Wade picked his pen back up and wrote one word.

Why?

Things were finally starting to make sense to him.

Meaning to Ask

Wade deliberately took a long time to build his qualification framework.

He wasn't procrastinating. He wanted it to reflect his honest work, and he didn't feel he gave it honest attention by rushing through it. He spent multiple evenings at the kitchen table after the girls went to bed building it. He would spend breaks between showings and client meetings at coffee shops refining it. He finalized it one Saturday morning while Kelli created a drawing and matching story about unicorns and Peyton took Amelia to a soccer practice.

The legal pad that documented his work was getting thick. The first pages, the complaint list, raw and graceless, softened at the edges from handling. The middle pages held the pipe, the numbers, the bottleneck circled in black ink. Then the cloud, the assumption, the X. And now, on the last three pages before the cardboard back, the qualification framework. Twelve questions, organized by stage, written and rewritten until the handwriting was small and tight and certain.

He was proud of it, and he felt the pride was justified. He thought he was proud of Esteban's presentation. He came to realize that wasn't pride. It was relief. This wasn't perfect, and Wade was positive that Terry would have opinions on how it might work. He accepted that. The framework was specific, honest, and his. He concluded that is what mattered most.

Wade's drive to Terry's office was becoming routine for him. He found himself excited to make the drive, too. Each time he passed the exit he would have taken to Turner & Associates, he felt less guilt. He enjoyed having coffee waiting at Terry's office, but he mostly enjoyed the calming nature of the space. The glass door, the plant, the photograph of the girl in the swimming cap. All of it reminded him that there are better ways to work.

"Morning," Terry said as he walked in.

"Morning." He sat down and set the legal pad between them, open to the first page of the framework. "Built it. Twelve questions. Three stages; initial contact, pre-appointment, and post-first-meeting. Each question has a purpose and a follow-up path depending on the answer."

Terry picked up the pad and read Wade's work without any rush. As always, she gave his qualification questions her full attention. Wade watched her eyes move down the page and across and down again, and he waited. He felt less exposed and more curious as to what Terry would say. He didn't wait for a verdict. He waited for what she'd see that he couldn't.

She set the pad down. Tapped the first question with her finger.

"Are you pre-approved for a mortgage?" she asked Wade.

"Yeah. That's the opener. Gets the practical stuff out of the way. Are they financially ready or are we working with hypothetical hopes," he replied.

"Why do you need to know that?"

Wade knew this wasn't small talk or to test him. She leaned back slightly to study him while he thought about the question. But Wade was ready for this test, and he had asked himself the same question when he built the framework and again on the drive to Terry's office.

"Because I don't want to waste time showing houses to people who can't buy," he said. Reasonable. Obvious. The kind of answer that would have earned a nod in Sam's office and moved things along.

"Why would that waste your time?" Terry immediately asked again.

"Because if they can't get financing, the deal falls apart. I do all this work and it collapses at the last step," Wade responded. Again, a question he had asked himself and expected from Terry.

"Why is that different from any other lead that doesn't close?"

Wade opened his mouth, paused before speaking, and closed it. This question he hadn't thought of or prepared for. It was less obvious than the other two, and he had to sit with it before answering. Wade saw Terry grin as he started to think about the answer, knowing full well this is what she intended. He gave Terry a puzzled look in response.

He invested time in deals that fell apart for other reasons. Buyers changed their minds. Sellers pulled listings. Inspections revealed deal-breakers. People who just didn't want to work with him. Those stung, but they didn't carry the same charge. If buyers couldn't finance their purchase, they wouldn't need to be looking.

"It feels like I should have known," he said slowly. "Like I could have prevented it. When I lose other deals, it's just bad luck. But when someone can't get a mortgage, it feels like I was careless and should have known better."

"Why does that feel like carelessness rather than just an incomplete process?"

Another question he wasn't prepared to answer. Now he was thinking about something that didn't really matter to the qualification process. Or did it? He wasn't talking about pre-approval anymore. He wasn't even talking about financing in a general sense. He was talking about something deeper, the feeling of having been foolish and not working with serious buyers.

"I want to know if they're serious," Wade said. "I need to know they've taken a concrete step. Pre-approval is just—it's the easiest thing to check. I really just want to know whether they're just thinking about buying a property versus actually wanting to take action. I guess it's just the best proxy for that."

"Why use a proxy instead of just asking?"

Yet another why question. Wade hadn't thought this way when evaluating his framework, but he also didn't know why Terry was pushing him so hard. He asked himself if the client was involved in the process. He asked himself repeatedly if he was making an assumption about their motivations. He never asked himself to explain why his thinking about the process was built as it had been. Wade took his time and looked at the floor again as he ran the question through his head. Terry let him take his time with the room in complete silence.

Wade finally said, "I'm showing them respect as buyers. They better well respect my time as their agent. I can't keep abandoning my family, and I won't give up my time with them for people who aren't as committed to a positive end as I am." Wade stared directly at Terry, realizing why she had pushed so hard with more and more questions. She was helping him investigate and understand the purpose of each question in his framework.

Terry stood up, walked to the whiteboard, and wrote three words in her clean, blocky handwriting.

5 WHYS

She underlined it once.

"That's the technique," she said. "You wrote *Are you pre-approved for a mortgage?* What you meant was *I need to know you'll respect my time the way I'll respect yours.* Those aren't the same question. The first one is a yes-or-no with a polite answer. The second one is the actual conversation." She tapped the board. "The first answer to the first why is almost never the foundational thinking. The second one is closer. By the fifth, you're usually somewhere true."

Wade looked at the legal pad. Then at the board. Then at a call he kept replaying.

"I never asked Esteban one real question," he said quietly. "I asked him things. But every single thing I asked was downstream of something I'd already decided about him. Sixty-three slides were me answering questions he never got to ask."

"You skipped the why entirely. Five times over." Terry let it land. Then she sat back down. "Pick another one. Let's run it again."

Wade flipped to the next question. *What's your budget?*

Two questions in, he was no longer asking about a number. He was asking what kind of life the person was trying to buy themselves into. Three whys in, he was asking what they were trying to be closer to, or further from. Terry let him work it.

They moved through the rest the same way.

Asking about a neighborhood was almost always coming down to commutes or proximity to important things, but Wade discovered it was more about what the person wanted their week to look like. By the eighth question Wade was filling the margins before Terry even finished asking. By the twelfth he'd stopped writing in lines and was writing in spirals around what he'd already crossed out.

When they had worked through all twelve, the page was unrecognizable. Arrows pointing at obliterated lines. New phrasings written sideways in the gutter. Wade's careful, certain handwriting from that morning had been overwritten with something looser. They didn't look like qualification questions anymore. They looked like the beginning of conversations.

"What's different about what you have now?" Terry asked.

Wade compared his messy product that made so much more sense to him. The original twelve questions were neat and well organized. They followed a logical path. And they were completely impersonal. He was conducting an interview, not participating in a conversation.

The revised version was messier. His questions were asking for potentially messy conversations. They wouldn't be easy to have with some people. Wade would need to trust his clients enough to let them choose how much to share, and to hear him when he expressed his needs. He had to trust them to engage the process as much as he did.

"The old questions were about me," he said. "But really, they weren't. I am okay with spending time away from Peyton and the girls — Peyton would be okay with it — if someone was really being helped. I don't know what someone's Peyton is, but they have to have one, right?" He asked Terry the question rhetorically. She nodded in agreement.

"That's how it works. When you understand someone's motivation, you understand their readiness. When you understand their readiness, you know how to serve them. And when you know how to serve them, qualification takes care of itself. The people who aren't ready will tell you, and the people who are will feel understood enough to trust you." Terry picked up her coffee. "Your father knew that. Every one of those journal entries was about people. His service sold itself."

Terry stood up and walked back to the whiteboard. She cleaned the space beneath *5 WHYS* and wrote underneath it in the same blocky hand:

Asking good questions will cost me clients.

She turned to face him.

"That's the assumption we changed last time. We named it. Now we're going to take the same technique and run it on the assumption itself. We didn't actually test it. We just agreed it was untested. That's not the same thing as knowing it's wrong."

Wade shifted in his chair. The exercise on the framework had been minor surgery — twelve questions, all his, all rewritable. The assumption was the floor of his office. The floor of an industry.

"Why would leads not want to be asked these questions?" Terry asked.

"Because they're hard to answer. Nobody else is asking them," Wade answered.

"Why are they so hard to ask?"

Wade noticed the shift in focus, and took a breath to thoughtfully answer. "They're not really about real estate. They're personal. People are hiring an agent, not a therapist. They'd feel put on the spot."

"Why shouldn't this process be therapeutic?"

He thought about every buyer he'd ever worked with. None of them had arrived expecting a real conversation. If he was honest with himself, too, he didn't really like them enough to have one.

They'd arrived expecting a process — show me listings, write the offer, get me the keys — but so did he.

"Therapy is terrifying," Wade said. "Real estate agents are crazy people. How are we in any way qualified to help someone through their emotional troubles? Everything we're taught is about protecting the client, but we assume the only thing they need to be protected from is malfeasance or incompetence. We never even ask how much they need to be protected from bad decisions they make. That's a very, very hard conversation to have with someone. It could take a lot of time unpacking all of that."

"Should they have that protection?"

Another different probe. Wade sat with it.

"Yes," he said. "Of course they should. But —"

"Then why doesn't anyone do it?"

The room was quiet. Wade looked at the whiteboard. He thought about Sam's whiteboards. The dashboards. The monthly meetings full of metrics. The whole architecture of the office built around what could be counted.

"That can't be measured," he said slowly. "You can count transactions. You can't count whether someone felt protected. The whole system is built around what can be tracked, because what can be tracked can be sold. It's almost impossible to sit down and monetize your ability to have a conversation. Nobody in the system says it. Everything is built on the assumption that real estate is just a transaction at the end of the day. We preach how important people are and how it's a people business, but we ignore people at the core."

Terry didn't write anything down. She didn't speak. She let the sentence sit.

"And why have you accepted that?"

Wade looked at the floor. Then at his hands. Then at the legal pad on the table, full of his own handwriting from a morning that already felt like it had happened to someone else. He had never asked himself this question.

"Because everyone around me has."

Terry waited.

He thought about it longer. About Sam standing in front of the bullpen. Jordan in the hallway with the shoulder clap. Sloan with her morning coffee and her perfect nails. The clients who came in already expecting a transaction. The years he'd spent putting on what he now realized was a hat — agent-Wade, the one who hustled and executed and didn't get sentimental — and the other Wade he came home to.

"But my dad never did."

He said it quietly. The words came out before he was ready for them. He sat with them. Then he said it again, more steadily.

"My dad never did. He didn't have a business hat and a person hat. There was just him. It was a core of his business that he remembered people's life stories, and he never separated the two. For him, you couldn't. Business was personal because everything was personal. He didn't have the language for any other way to do it."

The room held still. Terry let the silence sit longer than Wade expected.

Then, quietly, she said, "Our moments with people are gifts, and those gifts pay us handsomely if we let them. The reason the assumption that questions will turn people away is wrong comes down to the fact that willing buyers want that gift. They want to share it."

Wade's drive home felt lighter, even with the homework Terry gave him to finish before they next met. Terry had tasked him with finding all the reasons why he might not be a good fit for someone. She wanted him to think about the qualification process being important to both him and his potential clients. She encouraged him not to rush it, either, and she would let him have his space to complete it.

The notebook on the passenger seat held two things now. The original framework of twelve neat questions he'd been proud of that morning. Then, the revised version scrawled in the margins and between the lines. He stopped asking what he needed to know and started asking what the client needed him to understand.

Underneath was the fear of scarcity that had built his entire business in its own image, and the belief that propped it up: that business isn't personal. The two had reinforced each other for three years. The fear made personal feel reckless. The impersonality made the fear feel rational. He'd lived inside the loop without ever seeing the shape of it.

He still didn't have the full system. But he had a clear sense of what it needed to be. A beacon, not a megaphone. A signal for the people already looking for what he offered, and a way to walk them through the part of the process they couldn't navigate alone.

He pulled into the driveway at 2:45 PM. The earliest yet.

Kelli was on the couch with a blanket and a picture book, narrating the story to herself in a voice that was half reading and half invention. Amelia was at the kitchen table with math homework, her pencil moving with focused deliberation. She always wanted to get the questions right the first time. Wade relieved their daytime sitter and sat down at the kitchen table. He reached into his bag for the work he'd done that day with Terry. Then, he paused. He knew what he wanted the qualification questions to do, but the questions weren't the real work tonight.

He quietly pondered the last few months and everything that had happened. He started to apply the Five Whys to himself in all aspects of his life. He'd just used the tool to expose what the industry refused to see. Now he was going to use it on what he'd refused to see. He just sat with the question and let it settle. Amelia glanced over, smiled and waved, then went back to her math. Kelli's invented story reached a dramatic peak and she gasped at her own plot twist.

He thought about his father in the shop after hours. The composition notebook, the pen. Jon writing down what he'd noticed about the people who trusted him — not because anyone was paying him to notice, but because the noticing was the work. Not separate from the work. Was the work.

He told you. You just hadn't read it yet.

Terry's said it, but it was Jon's voice now. The journals on Wade's nightstand had been instruction the whole time. He'd been reading them as biography. They were just as much a manual as anything else.

He looked at his notepad. He looked at the room. The same kind of attention he was learning to give a stranger across a table was already in this kitchen. He'd thought there were two of him, one for out there and one for in here. There weren't. There never had been. The lie that had built his business had built that wall too.

He helped Amelia with her math. He listened to Kelli retell her story — a daddy dragon who came home to a big birthday cake, with fairies and goblins also in attendance. When they opened the cake, worms poured out of the middle and the dragon loved worms.

The evening unfolded the way evenings were supposed to: ordinary, full of small things that wouldn't feel important until later. He didn't check his phone until after dinner. He never opened his computer once.

Ordinary and important were all Wade needed that night.

HOME BY FOUR

For three weeks, since he and Terry last met, Wade started to turn people away.

He was never rude about it. He never slammed the door on people without another word. All he had were conversations, the kind he imagined his father had before writing in the journals. Where it made sense, he referred callers to other agents in the office and briefed those agents on what the clients were like. He also, in more than one case, told people they weren't ready to list or buy and promised to keep in touch.

He started immediately. The conversations went deeper than they use to. He asked, then asked again, until he found a deeper, real answer. He frequently referred back to the questions he rewrote in the margins of his notes, but often he found if he just let the conversation progress, they'd form naturally. He had opportunities to talk about his wife and girls, and hear about the happenings in other people's lives. Wade found himself just enjoying the long conversations with people. It made him feel whole.

Of his first five conversations, two leads went quiet. One said, with what sounded like relief, "Honestly? We're probably a year out. I appreciate you being straight with me." Another said he'd think about it and never called back. Wade let them go, but he did have them in his database. He made a mental note to ask Terry the right way to handle those types down the road, but his old relentless follow-up instincts didn't even surface.

The other three leaned in. One couple leaned in to every question like they'd been waiting for someone to pay attention to them. Another buyer remarked, "Nobody's ever asked me that before," when Wade started asking about an old neighborhood she lived in and why she loved it so much. The third went on for twenty minutes about his mother's health and the assisted-living search driving his timeline. Wade listened and understood by the end not just what the man needed to buy but why he needed to buy it immediately. He knew of an agent in the office whose father was also in assisted living, so Wade referred him over.

As the method became more intuitive to him, Wade's deeper conversations became more natural—almost by instinct. Every lead Wade qualified showed up to the initial appointment. Even the leads that Wade thought were better referred to another agent showed up to all their appointments. It wasn't scientific proof after three weeks, but the trend was positive.

When they met next, Wade couldn't help but feel that Terry's office started to feel more like home than Turner & Associates. The glass door, the plant, and the photograph of the girl in the swimming cap shifted something in how he thought about work. Wade started to question if Turner was the right place for him. The busyness was unattractive. He started to see the constant motivation by Sam created an overly aggressive, competitive environment. He felt overwhelmed just thinking about it.

"Morning," she said.

"Morning." Wade sat down and opened a second, fresher notebook. The first was dense now: layers of handwriting, early entries broad and imprecise, the later ones more specific. Front to back, the notebook carried Wade's learning but also showed its progression. In the new notebook, he mapped the three weeks in his own shorthand: leads contacted, conversations held, appointments set, appointments kept.

"I had twenty-one leads come in over the three weeks," he said. "I had genuine qualification conversations with thirteen of them. Four weren't ready. Some told me directly, some I could hear it in how they answered. I referred out three more. Six committed to appointments." He paused, because the next number was the one that mattered. "All six showed up. Even the referrals. I confirmed it."

"Twenty-one. That's lighter inflow than you used to see," Terry said.

"Yeah. Some of them I turned away before they became leads at all. The ones I knew I'd be chasing for nothing — I just told them what I do and they decided not to go further. I never put them in the database."

Terry nodded and set down her coffee.

"Your old conversion rate from first contact to kept appointment was around four percent. This was over twenty-eight."

"Exactly. And the six who showed up were ready. Prepared before they walked in the door. Two already had pre-approval. One had already toured the neighborhood she wanted. They weren't browsing. They were buying. Some were ready to sell so they could buy."

"How did that feel?"

"Steady. Almost predictable." Wade set his coffee down. "I wasn't chasing anyone. I wasn't convincing anyone. I was just having good conversations. The right people stayed and the wrong people left, and both of those things were fine. And I actually enjoyed it, Terry. I really enjoyed spending time with these people."

Terry nodded, and expected a triumphant feeling to course through his veins. What he felt underneath was simpler: for the first time as an agent, he felt consistent. Terry's guidance had given him stability. His days were predictable, his work was fulfilling, and he spent more enjoyable moments with his wife and girls.

"You want this to stabilize for a good while," Terry said. "Three months, maybe six. Then you start asking what happens when you increase that pipeline. What happens when it doubles or triples. You can manage things now, but there will come a point where you simply can't do anymore on your own."

Wade's stomach shifted. The qualification conversations worked, but each one required his full attention. His voice. His judgment. His presence on the phone, listening for things that couldn't be scripted. He had no idea how to handle new volume without reverting to the old patterns.

"So you're telling me I should just keep going with conversations, appointments, showings, negotiations, active client follow-up until I am out of time again?" He did the math in his head and felt the familiar weight of it. "I still have a bottleneck."

"Yes," Terry said.

"So I'm still stuck."

Terry got up and walked to the whiteboard. She picked up the marker and wrote a single word:

Elevation

"You've done the first three things," she said, underlining each as she spoke. "You identified the constraint: the qualification step that didn't exist, and why it persisted. You exploited it by building a framework that turns every conversation into a genuine assessment. You subordinated your marketing, your follow-up, your time to serve that constraint."

She tapped the board and drew a line that gradually went up until a certain point, then she drew it near vertical.

"Elevation. Expanding the capacity of the constraint you've defined and exploited. This is where you start to see your exponential gains, and not by working faster or longer. By expanding what's possible without expanding your hours."

"How?"

Terry set the marker down and walked out of the conference room. She came back with her laptop, opened it, and showed Wade the screen.

"Tell me what you see," she said.

Wade leaned forward. A conversation. Text on a screen, back-and-forth between someone named Lisa and what appeared to be Terry's business. The exchange was warm, specific, unhurried. Lisa reached out about selling her home.

Terry's response asked what was prompting the move. Lisa explained that her kids had graduated, the house was too big now. She wanted something smaller, with a garden. The next question asked what she'd miss most about the current house. Lisa didn't respond immediately. The timestamp showed a gap of over an hour. But Lisa wrote back something about the kitchen where she'd taught her daughter to cook.

The conversation continued. Questions about timeline. Questions about what smaller meant to her. Questions about whether she thought about where she wanted to be. Each question built on the last. The tone was conversational without being casual, professional without being cold.

"You're really good at this," Wade said.

"I would hope so," Terry said. "I had to build the damn thing."

He looked at the timestamps. The first message had come in at 11:47 PM on a Tuesday. Terry's response arrived at 11:49 PM.

"You weren't awake at midnight, were you?" Wade asked.

"No. I most definitely was not," Terry answered with a laugh.

Wade stared at the screen. The conversation continued. A dozen more exchanges. All spread across the next two days, each one building understanding at odd hours. At the end of the two-day thread, Lisa had written: Can we spend some time talking through next steps? When works? The response offered three times, all within Terry's working hours. Lisa chose the one that worked for her.

"How many of these are happening right now?" Wade asked.

"Seventeen in the last week. Six are new leads in various stages of qualification. Four are follow-ups from conversations I had in person. Five are people who aren't ready yet but wanted to stay in touch. Two are clients who just completed a closing." Terry closed the laptop. "Every one of those conversations follows the same logic you built into your framework. Same questions. Same listening. Same respect for where the person actually is, not where I want them to be."

Wade sat with it. The thing on the screen wasn't a chatbot. It wasn't the robotic auto-responders he'd seen at conferences. The ones sending canned messages that scream robot in every line. What he read felt human because it was built on Terry's human thinking. Her decades of learning what to ask and when. She knew why it mattered to her, so she trained it into this conversational—thing. The magic of it was it carried her thinking forward while she slept.

"The tool doesn't replace your thinking," Terry said. "It executes the thinking you've already done. And it can only do that because you did the hard work first. The constraint analysis, the root cause work, the cloud. Without all of that, you'd just be automating your old chaos."

His experiences of the last year were aligning. Everything he'd been guided through by Terry—the pipeline, his bottleneck, the Five Whys—all of it focused on thinking clearly. The goal to see what is happening before trying to change it. Only now, after the diagnosis, after the root cause, after they built the framework did the tool make sense.

"So all of the things I was trying to do were just trying to figure out how to be messy faster," Wade said.

"Exactly." Terry picked up her coffee. "There's this idea that says business owners need to scale themselves out of a job. An entrepreneurial coach named Dan Sullivan says it's important to ask 'Who, not How' and I agree. But, I say the how we think is incredibly important. The technology works just fine. When that breaks down or isn't an appropriate use, I have an assistant that works from home helping me stay in contact with clients and leads, too. She is fantastic, but we don't compromise on how we approach the business."

Wade thought about the vendor booths at every conference he went to. They all had powerful promises: automate your follow-up, generate leads while you sleep, close deals faster with AI. That's how he started using two of his CRMs because they both promised this very thing. The demos were slick, but it was like Wade buying a sports car to commute to work. Volume-based, fear-driven, unqualified pipelines were costing him money and time.

"We all just grab so many tools before defining problems," Wade said.

"The industry grabs tools instead of defining problems," Terry replied. "There's a difference. We assume we don't have to think if we hire someone or purchase the latest tech gadget. AI sounds like progress, but if AI is trained on bad thinking, it's just producing bad results faster. You will always have a bottleneck, Wade. Always, and that's actually a wonderful thing when you know how to think about it. You really can scale fast when you do."

He sat with it for a while. Terry didn't rush him. The office held its quiet.

Wade's thoughts drifted to his father. Jon Roberts didn't have fancy tech. He worked with composition notebooks and a pen. Everything he did was by hand. The remembering, the following up, all manual but entirely productive. He knew what Mrs. Elmer's grandson was studying in college. He knew Mr. Park's wife had a bad knee and didn't like climbing into the cab of his truck. He knew all about Esteban's business dealings. Jon kept all of it in his notebooks because those were the tools available to him. He was extraordinary at it, but the limit was him. His hours. His memory. His finite capacity for attention.

The thinking was the same, though. Terry's system and Jon's notebooks held the same understanding. People want to be known. Attention is the highest form of service. The question you ask says more about you than the answer you give to their questions. The tool was different, but the principle was as old as his father's handwriting.

"He would have loved this," Wade said quietly.

"I'm sure he would have," she said.

They spent time talking through how things worked in practice before Wade left. He asked about the thinking behind her systems, why she made the decisions she did. She corrected what he got wrong. He took a lot of notes. His notebook held sketches in shorthand, arrows and boxes, and the logic of a man who was finally learning to think clearly.

He understood, for the first time, what all of it had been building toward. Not just the qualification framework or the root cause analysis. The entire sequence taught him to think clearly enough that when the tool arrived, he knew exactly what to give it. What questions to load it with. What readiness looked like, in specific enough terms that something other than his own voice could recognize it.

The tool didn't think. It executed. The quality of execution depended entirely on the quality of the thinking that preceded it. Every agent at every conference who bought a lead qualification tool, and watched it fail, bought a tool. It was neither good nor bad, but it just was. None of them ever did the work Wade did with Terry. They tried to automate a process they hadn't designed. Worked to systematize a conversation they hadn't thought through. Attempting to scale something they didn't understand.

When Wade arrived back home and got out of his car, he loved the warm, golden feeling of the Georgia afternoon when the season was turning. Amelia's soccer cleats sat on the front step, muddy, placed with deliberate tidiness. Kelli's bicycle with training wheels lay in the yard on its side, abandoned mid-adventure.

He went inside. Peyton was at the counter with her laptop open, intently focused on the screen. She looked up and smiled.

"Good day?" she asked.

"It was," he replied. He set down his bag and sat in the chair next to Peyton. "Terry showed me something today. About how she runs her qualification process when she's not available."

Peyton's expression didn't change, but her attention shifted. She heard Wade talk about too many CRMs, marketing platforms, and services he signed up for and abandoned. She'd learned to calibrate accordingly.

"Don't worry. I'm not buying something else," he said, reading her face. "I think I already have most of the stuff I need. It's how she thinks about it. Her qualification process is solid and has purpose behind it. So when someone reaches out at midnight, they get the same conversation they'd get from her. And, she has an assistant that jumps in at the right time. Her clients are always being heard, regardless if she is available or not. It's pretty interesting."

Peyton didn't understand the concept. As a nurse, her job taught her to be on and available whenever she was needed. She needed Wade to answer with more detail. She didn't want to know theoretically what was possible, but practically what would happen as a consequence.

"What does that mean for your hours?" she asked.

"I don't know yet," Wade said. "What I mean is, I can't define that yet. I just need to make sure I'm clear on how I'm approaching the challenge. Terry called it elevation. I'm not ready for that step, though. I need to make sure my qualification process is consistent." He paused. "The bottleneck comes before the scale. That's the point."

Peyton closed her laptop. Not a dramatic gesture, her full attention shifting to Wade.

"Like what Terry does," she said. "Monday through Thursday. Home by early afternoon."

"Yeah. Something like that."

She was quiet for a moment. Wade watched her think. She was the ICU nurse assessing data, weighing it, deciding how much weight it could bear. Peyton didn't hope recklessly. She spent too many years in a profession where hope without evidence was dangerous.

"I'm interested to see it work," she said. "But, I have noticed you're not as stressed out as you normally have been." She took his hand and smiled.

"I'm interested to see it work, too," Wade said. He took her hand, stood up, and pulled her into a hug. Right there in the kitchen, they embraced. Wade didn't want it to end.

"The girls have a half day tomorrow. Amelia wants to go to the park. Can you be home?" she asked.

"I can be here," Wade responded with confidence.

"Promise?"

He heard the word and understood what lived inside it. Three years of broken promises. The accumulated weight of disappointment over being away, trying his hardest but producing nothing but stress. Wade knew that Peyton understood the broken promises weren't purposeful, but they were still broken. His work had been a system consuming everything because it had no boundaries, no constraints, no design.

"Promise," he said. The word felt different and he hugged her tighter. He was beginning to understand what it cost to keep it, and he was building something around his life that allowed him to keep the promise to his family and his clients.

Kelli came in from the yard, mud on her knees, three dandelions in her fist. She gave one to Peyton. She walked to the living room and gave one to Amelia. She came back, looked at the one she had left, and gave it to Wade. She only had three, but she didn't hesitate to give her last one away.

He took it, thanked her, and said, "Now let's go get you one."

They walked into the yard together, Kelli holding his hand.

THE APPROACH

Two weeks passed since Terry showed Wade the midnight conversation between Lisa and her AI system. As Wade sat there with her, he began to understand that the tool wasn't the thing. The thinking was the thing. The tool was just thinking with a longer reach.

He spent the first week building. This wasn't a scattershot approach like he used with Esteban's presentation. Wade employed a much more deliberate sequence of steps. He talked it through with Terry a few times to make sure he stayed focused. She suggested letting the process settle for a few months, but, he needed to show Peyton—and himself—this could work. After a few conversations over email and a phone call, Wade reached an agreement with Terry that he wouldn't fully automate everything. So, she talked him through a few steps and he felt ready to proceed.

He loaded his qualification process into the system Terry walked him through. He tested one question at a time. Each time, he made adjustments to the follow-ups to ensure the logic held. Branches in the conversation had to feel natural, and he wanted to make sure that the people on the other end of the line felt heard. Even Peyton helped him test it. Wade knew she would be hard to impress, and even she sounded surprised at how well it worked.

So, at the start of the second week, he let it run.

Now he sat at the kitchen table on a Saturday morning. The girls were still sleeping. Peyton was on a night shift that wouldn't end for another two hours. He looked at what the two weeks produced and printed out the results. Numbers on paper were real in a way numbers on a screen weren't. His father taught him that without meaning to. All those composition notebooks filled with handwriting that couldn't be deleted or scrolled past.

Thirty-one calls came in. The system engaged twenty-four of them. The other seven were after-hours inquiries that amounted to a single question and no follow-up. Just digital avatars of someone walking past a shop window without stopping. Of the twenty-four, the system carried fourteen through the full qualification sequence. Ten self-selected out. The questions helped them understand they weren't ready, and they said so. The system thanked them and offered to reconnect when the time was right. Four came through fully qualified: pre-approved, motivated by specific life circumstances, able to articulate what they were looking for and why.

Four. Out of thirty-one.

The old Wade would have panicked. Four was nothing. Four was a disaster. The old math that Sam preached in the office would have found a way to push for more. Wade was positive he would have asked how to find a way to connect with the other leads that never progressed further in the process. Wade used to believe that, too. He never knew which one would be the one.

Wade didn't panic. He ran different math. Four qualified leads in two weeks. All four booked appointments. All four showed up. Two moved to second meetings. One couple, relocating from Nashville with the husband starting a new job as a doctor, quickly made an offer on a house in Decatur. It was on the other side of

Atlanta, but they knew what they wanted and did the emotional work of committing to it before they ever talked to Wade. The qualification conversations helped them finish that work. They didn't need convincing. They needed clarity. The system helped with what it could while Wade focused on other things. When the system reached the limits of its capability, Wade came into the process.

His conversion rate from first contact to kept appointment was four percent. Two weeks in and it was one hundred percent of qualified leads. He knew the sample was small, but the quality of the sample was something he thought unimaginable. He walked into those meetings with a depth of understanding about the people across the table that he never had before.

At the next Monday morning meeting Wade attended, the brokerage had its usual frenetic energy. Phones ringing, Sam's motivational quote of the week taped to the break room wall—*Hustle Beats Talent When Talent Doesn't Hustle!* The hum of a dozen agents doing a dozen different things with no unifying logic connecting them. Wade sat at his desk, reviewed his week, and opened his laptop to check the system's overnight activity. Two new leads had come in, one at 11 PM, one at 1 AM, both already in the qualification sequence. He closed the laptop.

Jordan was watching him, but tried not to make it obvious. He sat at his own desk, phone to his ear, nodding at whatever the person on the other end was saying. But his eyes drifted to Wade twice in the past five minutes. Wade noticed because he wasn't distracted by all the commotion. He was relaxed, enjoying a cup of coffee, and just observing what happened around him.

When his call ended, Jordan set his phone down and leaned back. Pausing for a few seconds, he rocked forward to get out of his chair. He walked over to Wade.

"You're doing something different," Jordan said.

Wade looked up. "What do you mean?"

"I mean, you're sitting there like a man who knows what he's doing today. Your computer is closed. Your phone is down. You just look like you're trying something new," Jordan said. Jordan's voice held its usual polish, but something underneath had shifted. Usually he was dismissive of Wade. Today, he sounded legitimately curious. "Don't be detached, though. Don't let those contacts slip."

"I'm not detached. I'm just focused."

"Same difference, man. I'm not saying it's a bad thing." Jordan picked up his phone to check a notification, then set it down. "Whatever you're doing, it's noticeable. Sam noticed. I noticed."

"Is that a compliment?"

"Just an observation," Jordan replied.

After the sales meeting, Sloan found Wade in the parking lot.

She stood by her car, the always-polished black Mercedes parked in the same spot every time Wade was at the office. She had her keys in her hand but hadn't unlocked the door. When he walked past she said his name. The tone lacked the bulletproof confidence that was as much a part of her professional identity as the car. This wasn't casual.

"Hey, Sloan."

"Can I ask you something?" She looked at the parking lot, then at him. She looked like she had been crying, and her exhaustion was apparent. It looked like the cumulative grinding had settled into her bones. "I need you to be honest with me. No sugar-coating it."

"Okay," he said, confused but curious.

"Is what you're doing actually working? Or does it just feel more organized?"

At that moment, Sloan's facade cracked right in front of him. She was one of the top producers. Sam held her up at nearly every opportunity as the standard of what can be accomplished. She stood in a parking lot asking a third-year agent whether his approach to business might be better than hers.

Wade didn't pitch her. Sloan wasn't asking for a framework or a system or a recommendation. She asked a yes-or-no question, and Wade knew she deserved a yes-or-no answer.

"It's working," he said. "I'm not printing money, but things have been better. If I'm being honest, I just need to be home for dinner." He paused. "And I am, every night."

"I don't remember the last time I had dinner at home," she said. She didn't say it like admitting a sin, but rather an observation of her mental state. Wade almost invited her over for dinner that night.

"I know Terry finishes up her day pretty early and always takes Fridays off." Wade regretted bringing up Terry the moment he said it. He didn't want Sloan to feel she had to compare herself to anyone.

"I know what Terry does," Sloan said. Defensive by reflex, but her body eased after a beat. "I called her. She was honest with me."

Wade didn't know what to say.

"Terry suggested I talk to you." She looked at the asphalt. "When you started this with her—whatever this is—did it feel like admitting you were a failure?"

He paused and thought about Sloan's question. This was the pause Terry taught him to trust. He wanted to be supportive, but he wanted to be truthful.

"Both," he said. "Before I got into real estate I worked in a marketing agency. I made decent money, but I was always working. Since the girls were getting older, I wanted to make a change. I got into real estate thinking I could do well and still be home. When I wasn't doing well and wasn't home, I absolutely felt like a failure. After working with Terry, understanding why that happened was the first useful thing in my past three years."

Sloan looked at him for a long moment. Then she unlocked her car.

"That's helpful. Thank you," she said. "Are you able to meet me here for a bit tomorrow morning? I have a few more questions, but need to go."

Wade nodded yes. They set a time to have coffee at the office, then Sloan got into her car and drove off. Wade felt like she had opened up significantly just in those few moments they talked in the parking lot.

During lunch, Wade received a call from Esteban's assistant.

"Mr. Roberts?" the assistant asked. "Mr. Gabaldon wanted me to connect you on a call. Are you available to talk now?"

"Yes, absolutely. I'm eating lunch, so if he doesn't mind a bit of chewing while I finish up." Wade chuckled. The assistant did not.

"Please hold for a moment. I'll connect you two."

Wade waited about 30 seconds before Esteban came onto the phone. "Wade? I know you have been waiting for my assistant to call, but I wanted to make this call personally."

"No problem. Esteban. I'm just finishing lunch, but how can I help?" Wade replied.

Esteban paused before he started talking. "I won't take much time. I've decided I'm going to move in a different direction with my search. I apologize for making you wait on me to call back."

Wade immediately stopped chewing. He had been looking forward to this call, but for a brief second he felt paralyzed with fear. However, he steadied his mind and took this as the first real opportunity to give his new thinking a critical test.

"I understand, Esteban. I really let you down when we met. If I'm being honest with you, I would do the same in your shoes," Wade replied. Then, he took the risk and asked the next question. "If you're willing to talk a few minutes, though, so I can learn a little bit. Would you tell me what you were looking for exactly?"

Esteban paused again, this time for a few seconds longer. "I'm looking for land like my grandfather had. He bought sixty acres outside Guadalajara when he was twenty-eight. Everyone told him it was too much land for a young man with no money. He said the land wasn't for him. It was for the people who would come after him. I have money, but I don't have the land I want."

Wade listened to the statement. When Esteban finished, he was going to use that space as the natural point to ask the next question.

"How much time did you spend on your grandfather's land?" Wade asked.

"I grew up on that land. My father built the first house on the land with my grandfather by hand. Then, he added a courtyard. My mother planted a flower garden. By the time I was a child, we all lived together there."

Wade knew by his answer that Esteban wanted to have this conversation the first time. So, he pressed on. Wade asked about Esteban's memories. They included his grandmother making mole in the kitchen that opened onto the courtyard. He and his cousins played together constantly. Esteban shared how the design was intended to connect all parts of his family together, and how the sounds were what he remembered most as he got older. He said he felt free there, but always comforted being surrounded by family without being enclosed.

"And, that's what you're looking for here," Wade stated. It wasn't a question, but a confirmation.

"Exactly. I'm sixty-seven. My children were born here in Atlanta. My grandchildren are growing up here. I want them to have what I had: a place that holds generations. Not a house. A home that can expand to contain the people who will live in it after I'm gone," Esteban confirmed.

Wade thought he heard a sadness in Esteban's voice. It was similar in nature to what he heard in Sloan's voice that morning.

"Can I ask one more question? Well, two, including this one," Wade asked. Again, he chuckled. Like his assistant before, Esteban did not. "Why not keep the land in Mexico? It sounds amazing."

The conversation ran for two more hours. Esteban shared how his family eventually had to flee Mexico as violence spread. Having some wealth that grew with the land, his family increasingly saw themselves as targets and were forced to leave. After his grandfather had passed, his father made the decision to essentially give away the land for a fraction of what it was worth and moved the family to America in the 80s. Esteban, being in his early 20s at the time, felt angry at being forced to leave.

He wanted to try and recreate something like that here for his children and grandchildren. He wanted views from the hillside where his childhood bedroom had been. He missed the sounds of family gatherings across open spaces. His grandson loved horses and was learning to ride, so he wanted a place for them to pasture. None of what he described were architectural features. He described home, and the very essence of what it meant to him. He wanted to recreate a safe, more lasting version of what he had growing up and what he felt he was forced to abandon.

Wade listened. He wrote. He asked questions only when the silence invited them. As the conversation was drawing to a natural close, Wade asked for the opportunity to send him a few ideas.

"I can send them over," Wade said. "You can share them with the agent you start working with. I think it's the least I can do after I took up your time with our first meeting."

Another pause by Esteban. "I would love to see what you have. I'll have my assistant come back and pick out a time to meet. If you're okay coming back to the office."

Wade agreed. When he finished with Esteban's assistant, Wade sat with his notes taken during the whole conversation. He wasn't even aware of how much he had documented. It felt so much more tangible than the slides and book he prepared for their meeting. He felt like a biographer. Everything here felt like the story about a man that had never had the opportunity to tell it. This wasn't a client qualification. It was a human experience. Wade loved every moment of it, too.

They set a meeting for eleven days. Wade did not panic, but he did call Terry as soon as he got into his vehicle to drive home. They talked through the stories that Esteban shared, the questions Wade asked, and the feelings he had hearing Esteban's answers. Terry talked him through some suggested tools he could use to help do some of the property research. She shared some names with land experts that would provide guidance on what to look for and where to look for it. Most of all, Terry reminded him the constraint doesn't change just because of the size of the deal. She said the amount of money involved isn't even remotely important.

Through the next week, Wade did have some conversations with those land experts and did some research. He visited a few properties, and so his time driving he spent recording his thoughts on voice memos to ensure he was both safe and thorough. The night before the presentation, Wade sat in the living room with his laptop closed on the coffee table since 6:00 PM. Amelia was beside him with a book she was pretending to read while she worked up the courage to say something. She had a question and was deciding whether it was safe to ask. He could feel it.

"Daddy?"

"Yeah, bug."

"Are you nervous? For tomorrow?" she asked.

He looked at her. She watched more carefully than he realized.

"A little. Yeah," he answered.

"Why?"

"Because it matters. Because I want to do a good job for some-one I care about."

She thought about it. When processing information, she always tilted her head slightly. Her eyes would stare up and out so she could focus on her thoughts without distraction. Peyton constant-ly told Wade he did the same thing.

"Who?"

"You. Mommy. Kelli, if she's interested." Amelia laughed.

"You told Mommy you're doing it different this time. Sim.. . simatically?" She sounded out every syllable to the mispro-nounced word.

"Systematically. Yeah."

"What does that mean?"

Wade didn't want to give her a description of everything he did with Terry: the Five Focusing Steps, the constraint, asking why questions. Amelia didn't ask for a framework, though. She was asking for something she could understand.

"It means instead of trying to always be busy and feeling scared I'm not doing it right, I only try to figure out how to do the most important things right. So I practiced and I stopped worrying about all the other things."

"Like when I do my math homework and Ms. Patterson says do the hard problems first and the easy ones go faster?" Amelia intuitively understood the answer.

"Kinda like that, " Wade confirmed.

"That's smart, Daddy."

"Ms. Patterson is smart."

"You're smart too," she said, with the total certainty of someone who never considered the alternative. "And you're a good daddy."

He put his arm around her, and she leaned into it. She went back to her book. He sat with her. The evening was quiet.

Kelli appeared in the doorway in her pajamas, outraged at not being included in whatever was happening on the couch. She demanded a story. Wade improvised one involving a dolphin named Gerald building an underwater mansion. Gerald's friends didn't trust the human contractor he hired. It was a complete nonsense story, but Kelli declared it the best she ever heard. She declared that about most stories. Wade put them both to bed, tucked them both in, and kissed his daughters goodnight.

Wade knew this wasn't possible a few months ago. The previous presentation confirmed that. At this moment, though, he felt both calm and unstoppable. He was confident in the work he put in, but he was also calm about knowing that it mattered less than continuing that conversation with Esteban.

He walked to the kitchen. Peyton looked up.

"Girls are down," he said.

"You told them that dolphin story?"

"Gerald had character development this time." She smiled at the thought.

"Ready for tomorrow?" she asked.

"I am."

"Good," Peyton replied, looking at him with a mix of admiration, appreciation, and forgiveness.

Wade stood in his kitchen late on a Thursday night, rested and ready and home.

When tomorrow came, he would be just fine.

Facing West

Wade woke before the alarm at about 5:45 AM.

He wasn't in a panic. He slept soundly, and surprised himself the night before when he went to bed a bit earlier than normal. He didn't have the emergency alarm through his body like the first time he met with Esteban. Cortisol was replaced with calm.

The bedroom was still dark. Peyton asleep beside him. So, Wade lay in bed listening to the house breathe. The ticking of a clock came through the wall. The ever-running kitchen appliances hummed down the hall. He heard Kelli making sounds in her room, which he assumed was her talking in her sleep.

His presentation to Esteban was at 10:00 AM.

Wade was ready and confident. He built the presentation in the hours he chose. Closed his laptop at six every evening. Ate dinner with his family every night, and the presentation didn't suffer for it.

He'd found three distinct, but useful, properties. Each one mapped to the conversation with Esteban on the phone. He did prepare an appendix with numbers that he'd offer to Esteban when he needed them. But Wade understood now, in the way he couldn't have understood before, that Esteban wasn't buying numbers. He was building a safer version of the life for his family than his grandfather built for him.

Wade got up. Showered. Dressed. Made coffee and stood at the kitchen counter while the house stayed quiet around him. Wade even enjoyed the richness of the morning coffee, choosing to read some sports news instead of reviewing his presentation outline again. Only after his wife and girls awoke, got ready for the day, and they were out the door did he start to think about his planned meeting.

The drive to Esteban's office took ninety minutes, during which Wade vocally asked himself questions Esteban might ask. He played through scenarios and conversation branches. He thought about his father on the drive, too, specifically a journal entry he'd read the night before. Jon detailed a Mr. Nguyen's car for free because the family brought that same vehicle to Jon's shop for over a decade. He wrote that the service anniversary should be celebrated. So, they invited Jon to the daughter's wedding.

Jon wrote in the entry: *Showed up for someone who shows up for us. That's the business.*

Wade understood. Previously, he thought that just meant having good customer service. It wasn't. Knowing what actually mattered and directing finite energy there was the business for Jon. Jon didn't detail Mr. Nguyen's car because it was good business. He did it because the relationship powered the profits. The car was just what moved through the system.

Wade parked outside the converted warehouse. He sat for a moment with the engine off, hands on the wheel. He wasn't nervous. He took the deliberate pause that Terry took. He wanted one more breath to connect the work already done to the work at hand.

He grabbed his pad and his bag. Got out. Walked in.

After about ten minutes of waiting, a woman in a dark blazer appeared in the doorway to Esteban's office. "Mr. Roberts? Mr. Gabaldon is ready for you."

Esteban's office looked different than it had the first time. Wade was fully present to see it clearly now. Bookshelves were heavy with literary volumes in English and Spanish. The walnut desk showing years of use in its grain and texture. The light let in by the window wasn't just illuminating, but warming. The room was perfumed to smell like a garden of spring flowers. Esteban was writing when Wade walked in.

He stood when Wade entered. Like their first meeting, Esteban's handshake was firm, but welcoming. When he released it, he gestured to the chair opposite and sat down. The room settled into stillness.

"Thank you for coming again," Esteban said.

Wade sat. He set his bag down beside him, but didn't gesture to open it.

"Well, I should thank you," Wade said. "I appreciate you showing me some grace after we last met."

Esteban's eyes shifted. The faintest adjustment, easy to miss. His attention deepened, and he leaned ever so slightly back in his chair.

"Let's get started then, shall we?" Esteban said.

"Sure, but first, I have one question I kept coming back to after we talked," Wade said. "If I'm being honest, I made some assumptions about the properties I found based on what I thought the answer is. You never really talked about the architectural style of what your grandfather built. You talked a lot about remembering the sounds of growing up. I assume the acoustics were pretty amazing."

Esteban immediately leaned forward in his chair. He locked eyes with Wade as he answered.

"They were. My mother was an amazing singer, too. In particular, I remember slow, sad songs that she would sing. Just the sound of her voice, and nothing else. It carried because of that courtyard," Esteban shared. For another hour, they talked about stories of him growing up in Mexico. When he thought of his grandmother's mole, he would think of the chile garden and how hard he worked to help grow the chiles she used. Talking more about his mother's music—particularly the way she sang—led into a story of his cousin that had been lost shortly before they left Mexico. Esteban shared happy moments, and he shared moments of heartbreak.

"Esteban, I can't imagine how complex all that feels," Wade said. "I mean, I've had a real hard time after my dad passed a few years back, but I seem to be finding my wife and girls again. We never had to go through all of that, though."

The past hour was heavy and deep. None of it talked about real estate, and Wade saw the weight of the conversation on Esteban. He didn't reply directly to Wade's last comment.

"Show me what you've found," Esteban said. He gestured for Wade to quickly transition to the presentation.

Wade opened his laptop to show the three options he found. Wade chose each because they all provided something that Esteban clearly wanted, but they also presented challenges. None of them were perfect fits, but Wade stopped looking. As he suspected coming into the meeting, Esteban's connection to what he eventually purchased was much deeper than they had spoken about on the phone.

"The first," Wade said, turning the screen so they could both see it. "A horse farm in Milton. Spanish-influenced main house, three outbuildings arranged around a central courtyard the current owners used for events. The courtyard is open-air. I asked the agent about the acoustics and from what they described, the sound carries the way you talked about. Twenty-two acres, mostly fenced pasture. Room for horses. The main house is four thousand square feet, but the outbuildings could be converted. Maybe a casita for visiting family, a workshop, whatever the property needs to become."

Esteban nodded as he consumed the description. He asked a few questions before Wade clicked to the next slide.

"The second. An estate in foreclosure. The previous owners modeled it on a Mexican hacienda. Fountain courtyard, open-air corridors connecting the wings, terra cotta and stucco. Twenty-eight acres with a ridge and strong afternoon sun. The bones are extraordinary. The maintenance was neglected for two years, so there's work to be done. The architecture is fairly close to that old Mexican style than most of what's on the market now. Good bones, but there will be a lot of work."

He paused before the third. This was the one that mattered. It wasn't the highest-commission option, but he felt it was the best fit for what they talked about. Especially after what Esteban shared this morning, this property was the best option for him.

"The third. Raw land. Forty-seven acres on a ridge past Buchanan. No structures. The parcel faces west. With the right building plan, the light would be direct and intense in the afternoon. At dusk, you a direct view of the sunset. The topography is gentle enough for horses on the lower acres and elevated enough on the ridge for a home that would see thirty miles of sky. It's a blank canvas, though, which means it will be the toughest in the short term. Long term, though, there's something amazing waiting there I think."

He turned the laptop toward Esteban.

"Each of these could work," Wade said. "Each one has something real to offer, and each one has real challenges. But there are genuine options here."

Esteban studied the screen. Then he studied Wade.

"Which would you choose?" he asked. "If you were me."

The old Wade would have reached for the safest answer that closed the sale. Wade knew what he wanted, though. He caught himself a couple times thinking through how he'd build out the property if it were his. He decided to share that with Esteban at that very moment.

"Property three," he said. "The raw land. If I'm being honest, I got a little caught up in dreaming about it myself when I was preparing for today."

Esteban's expression didn't change. "Why?"

Wade held the older man's gaze. "You can't recreate what your family lost. It's gone, and it's heartbreaking. I think you know that, as hard as it is to accept. The first two properties are good. Either one could serve your family well. But they were built for someone else and you'd have to adapt to that. Your grandfather did something he wasn't supposed to do and built something he wasn't supposed to build. I think what's best is inspiration, not duplication. You'd build from the land up, the way he did. The sights, sounds, smells—they'll all be different. But, they'll be yours to share with your family like he shared with you."

He let the words have their space.

"You shouldn't be in a hurry, here," Wade said. "I think we both agree you don't have to worry about this property being lost the way your family's estate was back in Mexico. Be deliberate, but if you want my recommendation, be deliberate and build something that is your family's and theirs alone."

The room was completely quiet. Esteban sat with what Wade said, staring at him intently. As uncomfortable as the silence was to Wade, he sat and absorbed it. But Esteban needed this moment, and Wade didn't want to abandon him in it.

"Your father would be proud of you," Esteban said, breaking the silence.

The words unlocked something. Grief, gratitude, and something like triumph, braided so tightly Wade couldn't separate them. He felt his throat tighten and didn't fight it. He just felt it.

"Not because of this," Esteban continued. His voice was quiet and precise and held the warmth of a man who chose his words the way other people chose what to build. "You understand what matters. Your father was a good man, and the best businessman I knew. He used to tell me: the car is just the reason they walked in. My job is to understand why they stay." Esteban paused. "You know your father was one of my earliest business partners here in Atlanta?"

Wade didn't trust himself to speak. This wasn't in the notebooks. The journals recorded memories and people and moments, but a business relationship wasn't one of them. The room held its quiet, and Esteban let it.

"Thank you," Wade said, choking back emotion. "For telling me that."

Esteban nodded. Wade stood to gather his things, but Esteban stopped him.

"Please, if your day allows for it, let's have some lunch here. I'd like to share some things about your father," Esteban said. Wade said he had to take care of a few things first, and Esteban picked up his office phone to talk with his assistant. His exchange was in Spanish, so Wade had zero understanding of what they were talking about.

Forty-five minutes later, lunch arrived in the conference room and Wade turned his phone off. He'd spent the time beforehand letting Peyton know he might be a bit late this evening after updating her about the meeting. He called a client that was patiently waiting for the meeting to conclude, and answered a few emails. After that, he wanted to be in the moment with Esteban.

They talked all afternoon about how Esteban arrived with some money to Atlanta, but had zero idea what to do with his life. His dream growing up had been to use the land to produce tequila, as he loved how beautiful the agave plant was. He knew that wasn't an option, so he followed another cousin around to mechanic shops where they had settled out near Carrollton. One day, he walked into Jon's shop and asked for an application. Even though his English was broken, Jon enjoyed the conversation and hired him on the spot. Jon didn't own the shop then—he still convinced Cahill to take on Esteban.

For years, they worked together. Esteban recounted how Jon always asked him questions about his family's work back in Mexico. In some cases, Esteban would share an idea that Jon immediately implemented. Especially after Wade was born, Jon relied on him to run the shop for him when he had to miss time. During that time, Esteban saved everything he could. When a business opportunity came to buy a distribution business, Jon encouraged him to leave the shop and go buy it. Even gave him a small loan to bridge the gap between what he had saved and what the purchase would cost.

The man who bought the shop from Wade's mother was Esteban's son-in-law. He worked with Jon, too. Esteban had helped him get a job there after marrying his daughter. He'd had trouble in his youth and was struggling. He knew that being around Jon would be a positive influence and prepare him to be a part of his family better than working directly for him. He'd flourished so much under Jon's guidance that Esteban loaned him the money to purchase the business.

Wade spoke very little that afternoon. He was in rapt fascination at all these stories he never heard before. He absorbed all of it.

"I don't know why my parents never told me any of this," Wade finally said.

"Your parents knew you were different from them," Esteban replied. "Your father always said you were the greatest thing he did with his life after marrying your mother. He also knew you weren't going to be a mechanic."

After hours of talking, Wade finally told Esteban he had to go back home. They shook hands again, and Esteban would call him personally to let him know the direction he wanted to go. He was honest and shared that he had lined up meetings with other brokers and agents after the first presentation. However, this time together was helpful and Esteban was excited about what was really possible.

The call came directly from Esteban about a week later. It was early on a Monday, and Wade was reviewing his system's activities to see what needed his attention and which leads he needed to call. He had started working at home more often and away from

Sam's office. He enjoyed the quiet after getting his wife and girls out the door each morning.

"Wade," Esteban said when Wade picked up the phone.

"Yes sir. Good morning," Wade replied.

"I've decided." A pause. "I want to work with you on getting that land. I'm also going to need help with the whole process of building on it. I'm assuming you can help with that too. Can we do it?"

"Yes, sir, I think we can," he said. "I should be honest, though, there are things I won't be familiar with. But I have some folks I can work with on that and learn from."

"Good. I want to let you know, though, this is probably the most difficult option I was given. I'm going to rely on you a lot."

"Of course, I just need to be honest up front, though, about a few things." Wade said.

"Please, go ahead."

"I missed a lot of my daughters' lives the past few years. I was trying to work like my father worked. I just need to make sure we have patience through all of this, because I can't do that. I won't be able to help if you need me all the time, every day." Wade's voice was steady. He thought about this enough to say it clearly and directly.

"He'd want you to be present," Esteban said. "Like he always was. I think we can make that work."

Wade smiled and responded with, "Then, I'll get in touch with your assistant this afternoon about next steps. There's some paperwork we need to get done first, but I think we can do something pretty amazing here."

"Looking forward to it," Esteban replied and hung up the phone. Wade spent time talking to the transaction coordinator in Sam's office. Wade was confident she would be able to coordinate all the paperwork and administrative work with Esteban's assistant. He also spent some time talking to a few potential virtual assistants that were familiar with the CRM that he had consolidated all of his workflows in. He'd been toying with the idea of hiring one for a few weeks, and the deal with Esteban made it a necessity. By the time his girls were getting home from school, Wade had concluded nearly all of his work for the day and was waiting for them at the bus stop.

"Daddy! Can we go to the park?" Kelli asked as soon as they stepped off.

"Easy, easy," Wade said. He picked her up and grabbed Amelia's hand when she reached for his. "What do you think, Ames? Should we go to the park and skip homework?" Amelia smiled and silently shook her head in agreement. Kelli screamed in delight and wrapped her arms around his neck. She hugged him so tightly that he choked.

He left his phone on the counter. They walked hand in hand to the park at the end of the neighborhood. While the girls worked their way through every piece of equipment in sequence, Wade sat on the bench and absorbed the afternoon. Warm sun, quiet neighborhood, nothing urgent anywhere. He was present and had zero need to be anywhere else.

Wade let himself calculate the compensation, soberly, with the measured recognition of what it would mean for his family. The trajectory of his family's life was going to immediately change.

Peyton found them still at the park at four forty-five. Scrubs still on, hair pulled back, she was demonstrably exhausted from her day. She sat down on the bench next to Wade with a thump.

"I figured you might be here," Peyton said. "You didn't answer your phone."

"Forgot it at home. Esteban called this morning, so I spent most of the day getting the first steps lined up to handle the deal. I guess when I was done and got the girls, I just didn't even think about it."

She turned to look at him. She wasn't assessing him like she normally did. The exhaustion evaporated. She was excited at the news.

"He hired you?" she asked. Wade nodded yes and gave her a big smile. She wrapped her arms around him, too. Wade thought Kelli's hug was tight, but this hug completely enveloped him.

After the girls had exhausted themselves, they decided as a family to go to a local restaurant to eat. As a family, they talked about their days. Occasionally, Wade or Peyton would have to separate the girls when they fought at the table. Together, they went home and enjoyed a quiet evening.

The last thing Wade remembered about that day was how quiet and peaceful the house was when he fell asleep.

Monday Meeting

The news moved faster than expected.

Wade hadn't actively shared the news with anyone, not even called Terry despite his promise he would call. He hadn't posted anything on social media with a humble-brag about gratitude and opportunities. He told Peyton at the park while their girls played. And the office's transaction coordinator knew. That was it.

Real estate offices are small ecosystems, though. By Wednesday morning, two days after Esteban's call, the climate changed completely. Wade felt it when he walked in. Nobody gave him a raucous applause. He didn't receive congratulatory backslaps or handshakes. His colleagues recalibrated. They looked at him differently when he walked in. He tried to casually ignore it, but it made him self-conscious.

Sam found him at his desk before nine.

"Wade." Sam leaned against the partition with the particular casualness of a man who rehearsed his casualness. "Congratulations about the Gabaldon deal. That's—I mean, that's a big one. That's a career deal."

"Thank you. It's a good start."

"A good start?" Sam laughed too loudly. He didn't know what to do with the understatement. "Listen, I've been thinking for Monday's sales meeting. Would you be willing to share what you did differently? I know it's only a few days to prepare, but the whole office has noticed some changes. I think people would benefit from hearing how you stepped up your game."

A year ago, Wade would have said yes immediately and hoped he had a week to build a presentation. He'd have rehearsed relentlessly, terrified of looking foolish, desperate to prove he belonged.

"What specifically do you want me to talk about?" Wade asked.

"Whatever you want. I'd be interested in seeing how you landed Gabaldon. Must have taken a lot of work. "

Wade paused to think about it. Considering they had only started this week, a lot was up in the air. Wade hadn't even had time to speak much to the seller's agent. He wasn't ready to take a victory lap.

"Sure," Wade said. "But I'm not going to talk about the deal with Esteban."

Sam's expression shifted. "No?"

"There's more important stuff to share about what I did before I even heard from Esteban. It was hard work, and the deal was just the result of all that."

Sam nodded. He looked like he regretted the offer for Wade to speak at the meeting, but it was already on the table.

Sloan found him in the breakroom that afternoon.

She was pouring coffee. She drank office coffee for twelve consecutive years without once bringing her own cup. Today, she had a nice oversized mug with the face of a man on it, smiling comically big. She was between showings, but Wade thought she was moving significantly slower than normal.

"Congratulations," she said. Sloan said it differently than Sam. It was awkward, but not because she was envious. It was said like there's more that she wants to continue with but stopped herself.

"Thanks, Sloan. That means a lot," Wade replied.

She stirred in cream. Took a sip. Set the cup down and looked at him directly for the first time.

"How much are you working right now? Hours, I mean. Weekly."

The question surprised him. Sloan never asked questions to begin with, but Wade never remembered her asking a question to anyone about how they work.

"Each week? I honestly don't know, but it's not a ton. If I had to guess, maybe twenty to twenty-five."

Her face was stoic like she was playing a hand of cards that could go very poorly if her bluff was called.

"And the Esteban deal. How long did that take you?"

"The first time when I muffed it was about fifty total hours. Second time was maybe five, six hours in total. Everything else still got done, though."

She looked out the window and shook her head. Wade wasn't sure if her reaction was to hold back ridicule or process information she didn't want to hear.

"I'm excited to see what you share in the meeting on Monday," she said. And walked out.

Wade was going on four years as an agent now. Sloan for decades. She's been the gold standard in this office for over ten years. He lingered in the breakroom thinking how much work she'd put into being in that exact spot so many agents—including him a year ago—would have killed for. Here she was, asking him questions about his work day.

Jordan was in the hallway. When Wade passed, Jordan looked up. The look was different. Jordan looked at Wade the way you look at a map when the territory changed and the old routes don't go where they used to. Curiosity: the kind that costs something to feel because it requires admitting you don't already know.

Neither said anything. Wade lifted his coffee cup and nodded as they passed each other. The silence between them was more honest than any conversation they'd ever had.

Monday came.

Sam sent an email beforehand: *Wade Roberts is sharing his approach Monday, don't miss it!* was the subject line.

Every meeting Sam played the part of a long-winded motivational presenter. Two parts bad advice mixed with one part good mindset techniques was the usual flavor. Today Sam kept it short. "Wade's going to share what he's been working on. Floor's yours."

Wade stood. No laptop. No slides. No presentation. He walked to the whiteboard and picked up a marker. It felt familiar in his hand. The marker reminded him of the thinking that had transformed him. He hoped it would do the same for the room. He hoped it did the same for everyone in this room. He held it for a moment before starting, and noticed that the room had more people than it could hold. A few of his colleagues, some he'd not met before, were standing along the wall in the back.

He didn't start with the Esteban deal.

"I missed my younger daughter's fifth birthday," he said. "I missed my older daughter's dance recital."

The room shifted. Monday meetings were about numbers and motivation. They were not about missed birthdays.

"When I missed Kelli's birthday, my wife told me that she knew me trying meant I wasn't going to be there. She went to bed that night thinking it was her fault. Amelia left me a sign on my seat so I'd know where to sit," he said. He paused, too, more for his own sake than for dramatic effect. With his voice shaky, he continued. "I was failing as an agent, but worse as a father."

The room held his words.

Continuing, Wade said, "My system was broken, and it needed to be fixed. I didn't know how to do that. Hell, I didn't even know if it was possible." He looked at the room. "I thought the only way to succeed in this business was to out-hustle everyone. The more you worked, the more inadequate I felt. I was wrong."

He turned to the whiteboard. Drew a horizontal line. On the left end he wrote Leads. On the right, Closings. In the middle he drew the pipe narrowing to a constriction before widening again. It was the same exact pipeline Terry drew for him. He spoke about how he chased unqualified leads and why he persisted so hard to push them through the pipeline. He talked about fear, assumptions, and how the culture had influenced him to ignore the simple and obvious problem he had. He talked about his mentor showing him a way to think—not a way to work—and how that resulted in him working less but still making enough money to contribute to his family.

"When everything is a problem, nothing is the problem," Wade said. He wrote it on the whiteboard below the pipe and double-underlined it. "There's always that one thing that actually limits what your system can produce. It's called the constraint. Identify it and you can act on it directly."

He set the marker down, then turned to the meeting room. He'd only spoken for about fifteen minutes. In that time, people in the room had moved to the edge of their seats. Eyes were laser focused on him and what he was speaking about.

"I'm not up here to tell you I've figured everything out. I haven't. The constraint moves, but I'll find it using the same process I used to find this one. When I elevate it, the constraint will move again, and I'll find the next one. That's how it works. It's not a destination.

You learn to think this way, and you get better at it the more you do it. Any questions?"

He looked at the room. Nobody raised their hand to speak. Sam, especially, looked incredibly confused. Or, was it anger? Wade knew his presentation wasn't going to be something Sam would have asked for, but he wanted it to be real and purposeful. Sloan, especially, was locked in on what he said.

People filed out in murmured conversation. Sam clapped Wade on the shoulder. "Interesting stuff," he said. "Doesn't get the blood pumping in the same way, but that was really interesting stuff." Then, Sam walked out of the room smiling and shaking his head.

Wade was erasing the whiteboard when a voice came from behind him.

"Excuse me. Wade?"

He turned. A younger agent stood in the doorway. Button-down shirt, sleeves rolled to the forearms, the slightly rumpled look of someone who had been in the office since seven and hadn't noticed the hours accumulating because everything felt urgent. He held a notepad with pages covered in handwriting Wade recognized immediately. It looked like his own. Dense and scattered, the penmanship of a man writing down everything because he couldn't tell what mattered.

"I'm Frank. Frank Morrison. Just starting my second year." He said it the way you announce a diagnosis. Factual, slightly apologetic, as if being in year two required explanation. Wade knew how many people quit within the first twelve months.

"Hey, Frank."

"That was —" Frank stopped. Started again. "Everything you described. The hectic hours. The scattered leads. The feeling like you're running in place. The pipe thing." He held up the notepad.

The page was full. "That's me. That's exactly where I am. I'm drowning and I don't know which direction is up and everybody keeps telling me to swim harder. Can I buy you coffee?" Frank asked.

"Yeah," Wade said. "Let's go."

The coffee shop was half a mile from the brokerage. Wade passed it a hundred times and never stopped. He never had the time to stop. Now he sat across from Frank Morrison at a small table by the window and understood that this was not lost time.

Frank talked the way early Wade talked. He listed symptoms in the verbal cascade of a man whose problems are so tangled that articulating any single one feels impossible. Wade didn't need to fish it out of him. Frank unloaded on the first person who let him.

"I have active leads, or at least what I'm calling leads," Frank said. "I don't know which ones are real. I worked last Saturday and last Sunday and I haven't closed in six weeks. My wife asked me last night if I was sure this was the right career and I didn't know what to say, because I'm not sure. I'm not sure of anything."

Wade listened. He didn't interrupt. He didn't offer solutions. He asked himself if this was how Terry felt when they started together. She didn't need to demonstrate she had answers. She just listened, understood, then taught to what Wade already experienced.

When Frank ran out of words, Wade pulled a napkin from the dispenser and uncapped his pen.

"Can I ask you something?"

"Yeah."

"Of those leads, how many are people actually ready to buy or sell in the next ninety days?"

Frank stared at him. The stare of a man who has never been asked that question. "I don't — I don't know."

"That's okay. That gives us a place to start," Wade said with a smile.

He drew a horizontal line on the napkin. Leads on the left. Closings on the right. The narrow section in the middle. Frank described his process, and Wade wouldn't respond with advice but more questions. As the process continued, Frank slowed down his answers and became more thoughtful. Wade noticed the tension in his body released as they spoke.

"It doesn't look like it's the leads you're bringing in. Sounds like you have some good ones," Wade said.

"I guess in the end, it says a lot about me that I can't really close a deal," Frank finally said. "Not to mention the income I can't afford to lose."

"There it is," Wade said.

"There what is?" asked Frank.

"You just said it."

"What, that I can't close a deal?" Wade motioned for Frank to keep going. "I guess if I need the income, that means I can't afford to lose a deal. And if I lose a deal, then that means I'm not really capable of doing this."

"You're getting there, Frank. Keep going," Wade said with encouragement.

Frank looked at Wade puzzled. Wade returned his gaze with a smile, waiting for Frank to land the root of his struggles. After about a minute, Frank's eyebrows eased and he said, "If I can't cut it, that makes me a failure. My wife says I'm too much of a perfectionist."

Frank looked at the napkin and the narrow section of the pipe. Wade could see it happening. The recalibration. The moment when a problem felt enormous and shapeless suddenly took a shape small enough to hold.

"So many people are harder on themselves than they should be," Wade said. "You're pushing yourself to close, and I'd imagine that you're trying to close so hard people are pushing back."

Stunned, Frank blurted out, "Can we meet once a week for a while? I can't pay you for coaching yet, but whe—"

"No fee," Wade said.

"What?"

"Someone helped me and never charged a dollar. I'll do the same. Tuesdays work?"

"Tuesdays work." Frank paused. "Why? Why would you do this?"

Wade thought about his father. He could give a long, winding answer about obligations and sacrifices. Never in his journals did Jon ever write the word sacrifice. Serving people wasn't a sacrifice he made. It was a choice between right and wrong.

"Because this is the business of how it becomes permanent," he said. "Teaching you the thinking is how I get to keep it."

Frank nodded, and Wade recognized what it meant. Wade gave it to Terry, sitting in her conference room, trusting this woman having no idea what he was trusting her to do.

When Wade got home, Amelia was at the dining room table. It was an atypical mess for his daughter. Construction paper, scissors, a ruler she used incorrectly were strewn about. She had her mother's precision but her father's stubbornness.

"Hey, Dad." She didn't look up. "I need help."

"What's going on?" Wade asked.

"At my math camp, we were talking about fractions. I have to make a poster showing them with pictures and I can't get the circles to be even. Mrs. Wilson said it has to be neat. Mine isn't neat," she said, frustrated.

Before Wade would have felt like making an impossible choice between work and spending time helping his daughter. Now, he immediately sat down at the table and forgot the world around him. His daughter was his sole focus.

"Show me what you've got."

They worked for an hour. Wade helped her trace circles with a compass, then showed her how to divide them into halves, thirds, quarters. The geometry was patient and specific. His hands steadied hers on the ruler. The two of them bent over the poster and worked as a father-daughter partnership. Amelia explained fractions to him as she worked. He loved hearing her talk. It didn't matter that fractions were basic math. Wade was enthralled at her depth and precision what she knew. He was grateful this was his daughter.

"One-third is bigger than one-quarter," she told him, coloring a pie chart with the careful precision of a surgeon. "Because the pieces are bigger even though the number is smaller. Ms. Patterson says that confuses people."

"It confused me when I was your age."

"Really?"

"Really."

Kelli appeared and demanded to help and was assigned the critical task of applying glue to the back of the fraction circles. She executed this with the liberal enthusiasm of a five-year-old who believed more glue was always better. The poster developed a slightly lumpy texture in the lower left corner. Amelia inspected it, sighed with the long-suffering patience of an older sister, and said "It's fine" in a tone that meant it was not fine but she loved Kelli too much to say so.

They finished at five thirty. Amelia held up the poster. The circles even. The fractions labeled. The glue, mostly dry.

"Can we put it on the fridge?" Kelli asked. She asked this about everything; her drawings, Amelia's work, even a sock she'd found interesting.

"It's too big for the fridge, Kel."

"Can we put the fridge on it?"

They all laughed together. Silently, Peyton came to stand in the doorway. Wade caught her eye and winked. She held his gaze for a moment, and the moment was enough.

Later that evening, Wade was at the table working on his computer. Peyton, fresh out of a shower and preparing for bed, came in and sat down.

"What are you doing?" she asked.

"Planning out the month." He turned his computer so she could see. "Work is here. But I'm filling in the rest of it first."

She studied the calendar. Her eyes moved across the entries: the soccer games, a date night, and blocked out family days. The work blocks, contained and reasonable, occupying their space without consuming everyone else's.

"You're scheduling life first," she said.

"Yeah. Work fits around what matters. Not the other way around."

Peyton was quiet. She was processing the full weight of what she heard. A year ago, Wade would have been frantic at the thought of keeping a calendar. Now, he was documenting the schedule of his life on it.

"Not too long ago you would have said that's impossible," she said.

"I didn't know how to think about it," Wade said. "I thought every hour I spent not working was an hour falling behind, but I thought working meant I gave myself more of a future runway to be a good husband and dad." He looked straight at her and said, "There's never anything left over when you do it that way. I think that's what I've learned the most."

She took the computer and selected a weekend on the following month. In the third week, she selected some days and typed.

Wade stood up and came around her to see what she entered.

Long Beach Weekend?

She added a question mark. Not because she doubted he'd say yes. She already knew the answer. The question mark was something else. It was the last remnant of lowered expectations. This woman learned to want things tentatively because wanting them fully led to disappointment. The question mark was her protection. She was showing it to him, and the showing was a kind of trust.

"Beach weekend," he said. He deleted the question mark and replaced it with an exclamation point.

Peyton smiled, picked up a glass of water from the counter, and paused at the doorway leaving for bed.

"I never asked—how did the talk go at the office?"

"Pretty well, I think. I met a newer agent named Frank afterward."

"What did you talk about?"

"Honestly, the same kind of things Terry and I did. I asked him the same questions. I didn't give him answers. I just helped him see his own."

"That's good. Sounds like Terry is a good influence on you," Peyton said.

"Yeah. She is," Wade replied.

"You'll be a good influence on him, then. Good night, my love," she said. And left the room.

"Good night."

Wade sat at the table for a few minutes after she left. The calendar stayed open in front of him. The month stretched out in squares, and the squares held the shape of a life he was learning to lead. Not perfectly planned, but very intentional.

He closed his laptop. Turned off the kitchen light. Walked down the hall and checked on the girls.

He was asleep before Peyton turned off her light.

THE RIDGE

The November morning was ordinary, but it had some teeth.

Wade poured his coffee in the quiet house and looked through the kitchen window. Frost was on the lawn. Amelia's soccer cleats sat on the front porch where she'd left them last night. Mud from the soggy game was caked and cracking on the laces. Some of Kelli's toys were lingering on the kitchen table where Wade normally did his morning work.

The calendar on the wall beside the refrigerator was full. He and Peyton agreed to buy a digital calendar they both patched into. It filled quickly as a result. Peyton added the bevy of family and children activities they needed to coordinate. Special shifts that Peyton had to work were marked in bright red. Soccer practices for Amelia were well documented, all the more important now that Wade had volunteered to coach. Kelli wanted to join a swim team when she discovered how fun swimming was without floaties. The indoor facility she attended was a good distance away in Cherokee County. However, days were intentionally kept empty with a simple block that said *OCCUPIED*.

Kelli appeared at the bottom of the stairs in her unicorn pajamas. Her hair stuck up and out in three directions. She came over, leaned her whole weight against his leg without saying anything, and announced into the side of his thigh. "I had a dream about a horse who could read," Kelli said.

"What did the horse read?" Wade asked.

"My books. He put them on the floor and turned the pages with his nose. He didn't really get them, though."

"Why not?"

"Horses can't really read. He was actually just pretending."

Satisfied with sharing her dream, she went to the pantry for cereal. She poured the milk herself now, with the deliberate ceremony of a six-year-old who had recently been promoted. Wade watched her without commenting. A year ago he would have been gone already, and the milk pouring would have been Peyton's small daily handle on the morning. Now it was his.

A few minutes later, Amelia entered the kitchen with a book in search of her morning meal. As of late, she had started growing ferociously independent and wouldn't socialize with her father until she was ready. She set the book on the table, then came back with a breakfast bar and an empty cup. After she poured herself some milk, she sat down and started to talk to Wade.

"You're drinking the dark coffee again," Amelia observed.

"I am," Wade confirmed.

"Are you going to drive out and see Mr. Gabaldon today? You always drink the dark coffee when you do."

"I am," Wade said to confirm. "I don't know why, but I just like it on those mornings. I guess because there's a lot of driving, I want to stay alert." He didn't realize she had been so observant. She nodded, then opened her book and started to eat the bar.

His phone buzzed with a message from Frank:

Are we still on this morning?

Wade replied:

We are. Will be short, though. Have to meet with Esteban.

From there, the morning proceeded according to plan. He drove the girls to school. The conversation with Amelia was brief and content. She was reading the second book in a series she liked and informed him, with the quiet confidence of someone who took books personally, that she really liked certain characters and not others. Kelli quietly sang to herself the latest song she had loved. When the car line chaperones walked out the school's front doors, they both said their goodbyes and ran inside. Each time, Wade wished they would just wait a little bit longer to leave the car instead of rushing out.

The coffee shop was the same one he and Frank had been meeting in for half a year. Same table by the window. Same two coffees. Frank was already there, calm and ready for conversation. Six months ago Frank arrived breathless and listing symptoms. Now he sat with the patience of a man who'd discovered that arriving early did not require panicking.

"Lost a client on Friday," Frank said before Wade had set his coffee down.

"Tell me."

"Well, let me back up." Frank shrugged. "I can't say that I lost them. We never really were the right fit for each other. After we spent a long time talking through why we couldn't get things coordinated the right way, they said they would feel better making a change. I agreed, and even helped introduce them to a friend of mine in another brokerage I thought would be perfect. Six months ago I would have spiraled all weekend. This time I just kept going."

"Why weren't you a good fit for each other?"

"They wanted a bit more speed than I could offer. My wife and I are trying to have a baby. The twelve closings I did this year were a lot, but they were good. Gives us plenty of time to try, ya know?"

Wade smiled. Wade had been there at a point in his life, too. He was happy for Frank and couldn't wait for those chats about fatherhood.

"How does it feel?"

"I'm good at this." Frank paused. "We bought a new Christmas tree to put up. It's not even Thanksgiving yet, and it just felt good to not have to argue about it. I had the time, we had the money, so we did it."

"That's the one."

"What is?"

"That feeling. When you stop having a reason to argue."

Frank wrote that down. Six months ago he would have nodded and forgotten it. They spent the rest of their time together talking about another client that Frank was trying to get a read on. On three occasions, Frank believed they were ready to list and the homeowner wanted to wait. First, it was his roof after his "friend" said that a new one might increase the value beyond the cost to replace it. Then it was landscaping to give it more curb appeal. This last time it was the holidays that made him want to wait, thinking nobody would be looking.

"Sounds like he's using you as a sounding board about whether or not it's a good decision," Wade said.

"What do you mean?" Frank asked.

"To me, he's not convinced he wants to move. Try asking him something absurd. Would he pack up and leave tomorrow if someone offered double his asking price? Don't listen to how he answers. Watch how he answers."

They talked through the strategy for another half hour. The pattern of their meetings hadn't changed since they began. However, they were solving more complex challenges by finding the simple solutions together. Six months ago Wade had to wait for Frank to dig through multiple layers before something honest surfaced. Now Frank dug through them himself and invited Wade to join him.

"Same time next week?" Frank said when Wade stood up.

"Same time."

Wade passed through the office on his way to meet Esteban. He didn't work there much anymore, but each week after the meeting with Frank he'd stop by. Most of his hours happened at home or in the small office he and Terry started to share. Sam still ran his Monday meetings with the particular gusto of a man performing a role he'd chosen long ago and could no longer step out of. The numbers had kept Sam from saying much about Wade's transformation directly. They were good numbers. Sam liked good numbers. He didn't know what to do with the rest of it.

Sloan was in the breakroom washing a coffee mug at the sink. The mug had a goofy face on it, a man laughing at something the world considered private. She looked up when Wade came in.

"How are you?" she asked, and meant it.

"Good. Just saw Frank at our weekly coffee. I'm a bit on the run."

"You know, you're doing some amazing stuff with that young man," she said. She set the mug on the drying rack. "You might be responsible for a lot of people doing things differently. Sam's a bit confused as to what to do with you. You okay with that?"

"I'm okay with that," Wade said with a smirk.

"I turned down a referral this week. First time I think I've done that without making up a reason." She said it the way you mention a small private thing that surprised you. "He wanted me because someone told him I was the closer in town. Couldn't tell me why he wanted to sell, though. I told him I wasn't the right fit. I gave him a name. It felt strange, but then it stopped feeling strange about an hour later."

"Whose name did you give him?"

She smiled and said, "Yours, actually. Let me know if someone named Steve calls. I know you're rushing out, but have a good day." She dried her hands on a fresh paper towel and walked out of the break room.

"You too, Sloan."

He passed Jordan in the hallway. Jordan was on his phone, pacing slowly. This was the way a man paces when the call is a conversation rather than a transaction. He looked up. Nodded. Wade nodded back. Jordan didn't break stride. The honest silence between them had become routine. Wade liked it that way. Wade checked on some things with the transaction coordinator, popped in to wave to Sam while he was talking on the phone, and walked out to make the hour-long drive to West Georgia.

Wade loved making this drive out to the construction site. The relentless congestion disappeared. People didn't drive aggressively, despite the two-lane roads. The road climbed gradually through scrubby pine and then opened into the ridge country past Buchanan. Forty-seven acres on a rise of land where the afternoon light fell through mature oaks in patterns. Wade enjoyed listening to Esteban describe his feelings about the property and show his vision through gestures about what was going to be built and when.

The foundation was poured. The skeleton of the main house rose from the ridge in steel and framing lumber. The courtyard was visible now in outline — the way the wings stepped back from each other, the way the light would fall through the open center in mornings and afternoons, the way the family spaces wrapped around the outdoor heart of the house the way Esteban's grandfather's home had wrapped around its own.

Esteban was there. He stood at the edge of the foundation in work boots and a jacket that kept him comfortable in these colder fall months. He turned when he heard Wade's car door close.

"Wade."

"Esteban."

The handshake was warm. They walked the property together. Esteban pointed out where the stables would go so his grandson could continue learning to ride. He pointed out where his wife had asked for the garden. She chose the spot herself, a flat shelf of land sheltered from the wind by the ridge but open enough to get incredible sun through the day. He pointed out the casita that would sit beyond the courtyard, where his sister and her husband would stay when they came up from Florida. The casita's footprint was small and deliberate, close enough to hear laughter from the main house but far enough to feel like its own small world. It was the same way his aunts, uncles, and cousins stayed close but separate at his grandfather's place outside Guadalajara.

They walked the framing of the kitchen. Esteban described where the table would go. He went into amazing detail of a custom-built oak table that wouldn't move once he's placed it. The morning light would come through the east-facing windows and across the table the way it had at his grandmother's. He had not realized, until he stood here a few months ago talking with the architect, that he had been carrying the shape of that morning light in his chest for fifty years.

They climbed up to the ridge and stood looking west. The sun was low enough that the oaks threw long, layered shadows across the cleared ground.

"Jon told me something once," Esteban said. He kept looking at the trees, not at Wade. "We were at one of my facilities. He'd driven a fleet repair out himself. After hours. Everyone else had gone home. He was sitting on the loading dock writing in one of those notebooks of his. He was there waiting for me as he said he would be. He'd actually been early, didn't want to bother me about anything."

"That sounds like him."

"He talked about you. You were maybe twelve. You'd had a bad season at baseball, he'd told me. Been benched a few times. He was trying to figure out what to say to you about it. He showed me the notebook. He'd been writing down what he wanted to remember to tell you."

"I haven't seen any of those notebooks," Wade said, looking at the ground. "But I remember that."

"I asked him why he was working through it on a loading dock, after hours, when he could be home. He said: *I figured out a long time ago, the work is what makes the rest of the life possible. But the work isn't where I live.*" Esteban turned. "Then he said: *Build the life first, Esteban. Then build the business around it.*"

"He never said that to me."

"He didn't have to. He showed it to you." Esteban looked at the framing on the ridge. "He only said it one other time. I always remembered it, though. I wrote it down. I didn't act on it for a long time."

"What changed?"

"I got tired of paying for the life I'm living. My grandfather never complained about what he lost, but I did. Even as I had my own family, I don't know that I did it the right way. A couple years before your father passed away, we were talking and he brought up the time on the dock. He reminded me to build the life first and the business around it. So, that's when I told myself to let go of Mexico and create something here. And, that's what you and I are doing."

Wade looked at the courtyard taking shape between the wings. At the place where two generations of a family would gather to make food and noise on a piece of land that belonged to the people who would come after them.

"I get it," Wade said.

"I know you do." Esteban put a hand briefly on his shoulder. He left it there only long enough to mean something. They stood without speaking for a moment, watching the light move across the trees. "Stay for dinner. My wife is making mole. She's been wanting to meet you for months. She's getting impatient."

"Sure, but let me check with Peyton first." Esteban nodded and proceeded to inspect another part of the build.

He texted Peyton to let her know he'd be home late but happy. She wrote back:

I'll save you a chair.

It was almost ten when he pulled into the driveway. The kitchen light was on. Peyton was at the table with a book and a mug. She looked up when he came in, marked her page, and didn't get up.

"How was it?"

"His wife sent me home with way too much food," he said, setting the containers on the countertop. "She made me promise to come back and bring you and the girls."

"I think we'd love that," Peyton said.

He sat down across from her at the table. Wade put his hands flat on the table and looked at them. They were his father's hands. He'd noticed that in his thirties — the same blunt fingers, the same slightly knuckled shape at the joints. Jon's hands had always been creased with grease. Wade's were clean, but the bones underneath were the same bones.

"I want to stay up a little. I'm going to write."

"Okay."

She kissed his forehead and went up.

He took a notebook from the drawer where he kept extras. It was leather, a deep cordovan red, a gift Peyton had given him on his birthday two months ago with a card that said *for whatever you're going to need this for.* He hadn't known yet, then. He'd left it in the drawer until tonight.

He didn't write a framework. He didn't draw a pipe. He sat with the pen in his hand and the blank page and listened to the house. Then he started.

The ridge today with Esteban. A few long moments of quiet, but then he told me my father once said build the life first. I hadn't heard that one before. I looked down at my hands while he said it. They are my father's hands. Different work, same bones.

He paused. Set the pen down and massaged his fingers. Picked it up again, and he continued his writing.

Esteban told me dad was on a loading dock, after hours, writing about me. I was twelve. I had a bad season. I never knew he wrote about me, specifically. I thought the journals were for the customers. Have to ask mom about where those are.

Kelli told me about a horse who could read this morning, except he couldn't really read. It was matter of fact. Amelia connected me drinking my coffee black with the days I meet with Esteban. If I'm honest, I don't know that I thought about it that much. My daughters amaze me.

Peyton wants to meet Esteban's wife. She amazes me, too.

His eyes were tired. So, he closed the cover. The leather was warm where his hand had been.

The house had gone quieter while he was writing. He sat there for a moment absorbing how serene the moment was. Complete calm and stillness.

He turned off the kitchen light and climbed the stairs.

Peyton was asleep, but she left her lamp on for him.

COACHES

Terry called on a Tuesday evening.

Wade was on the living room floor with Kelli, building a zoo. The zoo was Kelli's idea, but the architecture had been evolving since dinner. Kelli had decided the elephants needed a swimming pool, which required demolishing the giraffe enclosure to redistribute materials. The giraffes—now homeless—were standing on the carpet beside the coffee table in what Kelli called the "outdoor section." Amelia was at the dining room table doing homework with the focused deliberation she brought to everything.

His phone buzzed. He almost let it go. Evenings were family time. It wasn't a hard rule but a habit he'd built. But the screen said Terry Bass, and she didn't call in the evenings.

"Give me two minutes," he told Kelli.

"The elephants need the pool by the time you come back."

"I'll hurry."

He stepped into the kitchen.

"Hey, Terry."

"Hey, Wade. I expected voicemail."

"Building a zoo. I needed a break anyway."

"Good. I'll keep this short." Terry's unhurried voice on a phone always sounded like a person who had decided something before she dialed. "I want to build a training program. Formal. Structured. The Five Focusing Steps for agents. Workshops one Saturday a month, plus an ongoing coaching program for the people who want more. I need a partner."

Wade leaned against the counter. He could hear Kelli narrating something to an elephant figurine in the living room.

"Why me?"

"Because I figured this out twenty years ago. My version is from above the experience. You figured it out eight months ago. Your version is from inside it. The agents who need this will hear it differently from someone who still remembers what the water felt like."

He understood. He'd watched it happen with Frank. He'd seen it at a conference he went to in May, where two of the people who came to find him afterward did so because Wade had said his hours and his numbers in a way that didn't sound like marketing.

"I'm honored." Then, before old reflexes of always chasing a yes settled in, he said, "I'm also worried."

"Tell me."

"Life is pretty good. I built it carefully. Hours, family—there's always give and take, but it's balanced. I don't want that balance to be thrown off."

"Stop." Terry had heard the concern before, and had clearly already worked it through to the other side. "What's the first step?"

He almost laughed. "Identify the constraint."

"What is it?"

"My time."

"Then design around it. Not around what would be ideal. Around the constraint." A beat, then she continued. "I already designed the program that way. I'll send it tonight. Look at it in the morning."

"Okay."

"Go feed the lions."

The next morning her email was waiting. Wade sat with his coffee and read.

Wade,

One Saturday a month: a free CE class. Three hours. Twenty-five to thirty agents.

We facilitate. We don't lecture. They identify their own constraints. We hold the room.

Coaching program after the class. Group community. Async learning. $99/month.

Four hours a week of Zoom: two from each of us.

Enrollment, payments, follow-up: already systemized.

Roll in quarterly events as we get to 100 people.

TB

He read it twice. The framework applied to itself: the Five Focusing Steps used to design a program that taught the Five Focusing Steps. It was the cleanest thing she could have sent him. Built around what mattered.

He wondered what Peyton would say.

That night Peyton was reading in bed when he came upstairs. The girls were asleep. Kelli was starfished perpendicular to the mattress. Amelia slept under her tight covers with a chapter book on her nightstand and the bookmark placed exactly where the previous chapter had ended.

Wade sat on the edge of the bed. Peyton looked up. She read him quickly.

"Something's on your mind."

"Terry called. She wants to build a training program. A monthly class teaching agents the way I learned. Coaching program after. She wants me to be her partner."

Peyton placed her bookmark, closed the book, and set it on the nightstand. She wasn't going to read while this was on the table.

"Will it cost us family time?"

It was the cleanest question, asked without accusation. The question Peyton had earned the right to ask.

"One Saturday morning a month. Three hours. A few coaching calls during the week. Terry already has the logistics — enrollment, payments, follow-up — set up. So nothing else changes. That one Saturday might be an issue with soccer. Weeknight dinners don't change. Weekends that aren't workshop days don't change."

"You've thought it through."

"Some of it. Not all of it. I wanted to talk to you first."

She was quiet. He could see her processing. She didn't brace for the impact of disappointment. She was looking at her husband and trying to figure out, from her perspective, if this was an opportunity they would benefit from.

"Then the question is whether you want to do it," she said. "Not whether you should. Do you want to?"

For three years, every decision had been organized by fear, and the fear had made everything equally urgent. The quieter question of *do I actually want this* had not been allowed in. Wade hadn't realized how much that changed in him.

He did want this. He enjoyed his time with Frank. Although he wasn't necessarily coaching Sloan, their conversations at the office were so much more enjoyable. Sam even warmed up to his approach and asked meaningful questions from time to time. If he could have more of those feelings, he had no doubt how much more he would enjoy his career.

"Yeah," he said. "I want to do it."

Peyton picked up her book and opened it to her bookmark. "Then you should tell Terry yes."

She started to read. Then she added, without looking up: "And tell her I said it'll be nice to get you out of the house once in a while."

They built the program over three weeks. They worked on it together when they were in the office together. They mapped the arc the way they mapped everything by starting with the constraint and working outward. The first class would help agents see their flow and the impact it had on their customers. Terry said seeing was enough for the first month. Seeing changed what you paid attention to, and what you paid attention to changed everything else.

The first class met in a conference room Terry rented in a coworking facility, not at a brokerage and not at a hotel. Twenty-five agents. Tables in a U-shape. A whiteboard at the front, no logos, no sponsored tote bags. Wade stood there before anyone arrived and looked at the room. He remembered being a wide-eyed agent who came to a classroom like this. He walked out feeling like he'd been sold something instead of taught something. Although he and Terry would sell coaching, he had made it clear to Terry that he wanted this class to give them something they could tangibly use.

As the students came in and sat, he drew the pipe on the whiteboard. Leads on the left. Closings on the right. The narrow section in the middle.

"Somewhere in your business," he said when the room had filled, "the pipe narrows. One place. Not twelve. One thing limits what you can produce. We're going to find it."

They worked in groups of five. Each agent got a turn. Wade and Terry moved through the room asking questions. They never gave answers. Never named anyone's constraint for them. They let the questions do the work.

Walk me through what happens when a lead comes in.
Where does it slow down?
Why?

A woman in her forties, ten years in the business, found her constraint in the first twenty minutes and cried during the break. She had been carrying the weight as a mountain. It turned out to be a single knot. The relief came out as tears.

A second-year agent with anxiety attacks found his in two minutes and argued against it for the next fifteen. Accepting it would have meant admitting that most of what he'd been doing was wasted effort. Wade recognized the argument. He'd had a quieter version of it with himself, in a parking lot with a notepad, two years ago. Some constraints take a longer time to look at.

The agents who were doing okay engaged politely and took notes. They weren't broken yet. They'd come back when they were.

It was a quiet, deliberate three hours. When it was over and those who only wanted to earn their credits left, eight agents signed up for the coaching program. Wade and Terry shook hands at the door with each of them. He drove home in the late afternoon with the windows down and the radio off and felt, in his sternum, the specific quiet of having done something useful without performing it.

Three classes in, Jordan came.

Wade saw the name on the registration list before the day began. He wasn't surprised. He'd watched the recent shift in their hallway interactions complete itself: dismissal, then skepticism, then curiosity. Jordan in his pressed shirt with no tie, which for Jordan was practically casual, sat in the back of the U-shape and kept his arms crossed for the first hour.

Class proceeded normally. Jordan didn't volunteer to be the focus when his group's turn came around. He didn't ask questions of the others when they were the focus. However, Wade caught him three times not writing anything down and missing nothing. He knew Jordan was attentive and focused.

During the break, Wade made him a coffee the way he liked it—Wade had filed that detail somewhere a long time ago—and sat down beside him without speaking. The coffee on the table between them was an invitation, not a demand.

It took most of the break. Then Jordan said it quietly, looking at his cup.

"It's my name. I think that's it. I'm always so damn busy because nobody can leave me alone."

"Write it down."

Jordan wrote it. The handwriting was tight and managed, the way Jordan managed everything visible. The words on the page were rougher than anything he said out loud.

My name controls my life.

"Why?"

"Because everyone assumes I'm the same agent as the rest of my family." A pause. "My parents were a lot younger than I am when they started all this."

"Share it with your group when we come back. They're good people. Tell them why it's a problem and let them ask you."

Jordan nodded. Not the practiced nod he gave Wade in hallways for three years. A smaller, real one.

"Thanks."

"Glad you came." Wade put a calming hand on his shoulder and nodded.

Wade walked to the front of the room and watched Jordan from a distance for the rest of the afternoon. Jordan didn't hide and didn't perform. The constraint was visible to him now. That was enough for one day.

Months later, after a noticeably raucous class in which seventeen students eventually joined the coaching program, Wade came home to Peyton packing for their trip to Hawaii.

The suitcase was open on the bed. Peyton folded swimsuits the way she did everything. Each item placed without waste and tucked into its logical position. Kelli's came first — the one with the ruffled skirt. Amelia's one-piece with the dolphins. Peyton's own went in last, between the children's, the way she always packed.

Wade stood in the doorway watching.

"You're staring."

"I'm watching you pack for Hawaii."

"Same thing."

"Not the same thing. I'm thinking."

Peyton tilted her head down and looked up at him. A faint smile lived at the edges of her mouth. "I know what you're thinking."

"Oh, do you?" Wade said, with a wry smile of his own.

"Relax, sailor." She set Kelli's fourth swimsuit down, crossed the room, and wrapped her arms around him. He felt her exhale against his collarbone. She held on a beat longer than usual.

"You made this happen," she said into his shirt. "Don't forget that."

She was right. He had spent a year building a business that could function without him. Documented systems. Mapped processes. A virtual assistant who managed the inflow. Terry would handle the coaching calls he missed. Jordan agreed to cover anything that couldn't wait, a favor Wade had returned the month before when Jordan took his new girlfriend on her first trip out of town.

Two weeks. Hawaii. The four of them together. And nothing else.

Amelia appeared in the doorway with a worried look. She held the paperback book she had been reading as of late, but fidgeted with it as she came in. Wade took immediate notice and asked, "What's wrong, baby?"

"Daddy. Do you have to work when we're on our trip?"

"Tuesday and Thursday mornings. Thirty minutes. You'll all be asleep when I'm doing it. Otherwise no."

"Promise?"

"Promise."

She considered this. The verdict came in the form of a small nod.

"Can I bring four books?"

"Bring six."

She accepted that with a wide smile and disappeared down the hall.

A few days later, they were all relaxing on a remote beach on the Big Island. He hadn't anticipated the quiet. There were sounds—waves, palms, Kelli's running commentary on everything she saw—but underneath all of it was an ambient hum. Nothing was urgent. Wade thought he could get used to that.

He swam with the girls in the mornings. Kelli, almost six, treated the ocean as her personal swimming pool. Amelia waded to her waist and stood there feeling the pull of the current with the same expression she wore reading something she wanted to understand before continuing.

He took her on a sunrise hike on the third morning. Just the two of them. The trail went up through volcanic rock and thin vegetation, and the sky went from dark to gray to the gold that exists only in the minutes before the sun clears the horizon. They didn't talk much. Amelia was a noticer, not a talker on walks. She pointed at things without naming them.

At the top there was a bench. They sat. The sun came up.

Amelia leaned against him. Not because she was cold or tired. Because she wanted to.

"This is nice, Daddy."

"Yeah. It is."

His phone was in the hotel room.

He didn't miss it.

EPILOGUE

Wade was up the stepladder in the backyard with the pruning shears, taking the dead crown out of the smaller Bradford pear. His mother stood at the bottom of the ladder, holding it for the principle of holding it. The ladder didn't need holding.

He had been coming up every other Saturday for a few years now. The chores had taken on the feel of a ritual: the gutters in spring, the garage in summer, the trees in March before the bloom. The first few times he'd come, he'd asked what needed doing. Now he just walked the property when he arrived and made his own list. Wade always wanted to be there more, especially with it being five years since his father's passing.

"You missed a piece," she said.

"I see it."

"Mmhmm."

He cut the piece. Climbed down. Stacked the branches by the fence. The pears weren't quite in bloom yet, but they would be in a week, and she would watch them through the kitchen window the way she had watched them every spring since the year he'd started Little League.

She had lunch waiting for him at the kitchen table. She refused his help with the dishes the way she refused it every time. He had stopped fighting her about it. Doing the dishes alone was a way of being herself in the room with him, and he had learned not to take that from her.

He sat with his coffee.

"Amelia came home from school last week and didn't talk to me for a day and a half."

"Mmm."

"I asked Peyton what I did. Peyton said I didn't do anything. Peyton said it was just her being eleven."

"Peyton's right. It is just her being eleven."

His mother was drying a plate now, slowly, with a towel that had been hanging on the same hook since 1998. The slow drying was a thing she did when her mouth was getting ready.

"I'm trying to figure out how to be a father to a person who doesn't want me right now. Or doesn't want me on Tuesdays. Or doesn't want me when there's a friend named Sydney involved." He looked at the window. "I don't know how to be a stranger in the hallway of my own house."

She set the plate in the rack.

"Yeah," she said. "Having fun with all that?"

It took him a moment, then he looked at his mother.

He hadn't heard that cadence in this kitchen since his father.

Did you have fun out there?

Win or lose, every game, every time. His father had said it because it was the whole point.

His mother had taken what she wanted of his father and kept it.

"Yeah," he said. "I'm having a great time with all of it."

She laughed. The kind that comes out of a person before they know it's coming.

"He never knew what to do with you either, when you got like that. Eleven, twelve, in there somewhere. He'd come home and tell me he didn't know what he'd done wrong. I told him he hadn't done anything wrong. *Eleven is an age. It isn't a behavior.* That's how he responded."

"So, what did he do?"

"He just kept being your dad. That was it. He didn't always know what to do. Eventually you came back, and he was still there."

He sat with that.

He left mid-afternoon. She hugged him at the door. She held on a beat longer than usual.

"Drive safe."

"I will."

"Tell Peyton I want her here next time. And my granddaughters. I think they'll tolerate you being here, too."

"I will."

He drove out under the pears. The branches he'd stacked by the fence threw a long shadow on the grass.

He was almost to the highway before he realized he had left the notebook.

He could turn around. He thought about it. He decided, on the long open stretch of road with the radio off and the windows down, that it didn't matter. He'd pick it up next time.

Back at the house, his mother was clearing the table.

She saw the notebook on the chair where he had been sitting. Cordovan red, leather, the cover scuffed in two places from use. Her first instinct was to call him. Her phone was on the counter. She picked it up.

Then she set it back down.

She sat in the chair. She put her hand on the cover of the notebook for a moment, the way you put your hand on a person's shoulder to tell them you are about to say something you mean.

She opened it.

She recognized the handwriting as her son's. She had seen it in the margins of his school notebooks thirty years ago, in the cards he'd written her at Christmas, in the inside cover of every book she had given him as a boy and watched him refuse to part with. It hadn't changed, but it had matured. It was still her son's hand.

She read the first entry.

The ridge today with Esteban. A few long moments of quiet, but then he told me my father once said build the life first. I hadn't heard that one before. I looked down at my hands while he said it. They are my father's hands. Different work, same bones.

Esteban told me dad was on a loading dock, after hours, writing about me. I was twelve. I had a bad season. I never knew he wrote about me, specifically. I thought the journals were for the customers. Have to ask mom about where those are.

Kelli told me about a horse who could read this morning, except he couldn't really read. It was matter of fact. Amelia connected me drinking my coffee black with the days I meet with Esteban. If I'm honest, I don't know that I thought about it that much. My daughters amaze me.

She put a hand to her mouth, then turned the page. She kept reading.

The Bradford pears moved outside the window in the wind. As petals fell, she just kept reading.

AFTERWORD

The thinking in this book is not mine alone. It belongs to the Theory of Constraints, a body of practice with decades and thousands of people behind it.

TOC, developed by Eliyahu Goldratt and laid out across his books, is fundamentally the philosophy that a system is limited by a single bottleneck. That limit is not a bad thing. When you identify it, it makes improvements simple, focused, and highly profitable. *The Goal* introduced TOC to the world. *It's Not Luck* showed us how to effectively think in a TOC framework. The Choice was the philosophical underpinning of everything. For practitioners like myself, the *TOC Handbook* is almost biblical in its importance. Wade's pipe, his Five Focusing Steps, his Evaporating Cloud — they are all concepts and ideas developed by Goldratt in TOC, but specifically adapted for understanding and relevance to the real estate industry. To that, I will eternally owe gratitude to **Dr. Eliyahu Goldratt** and many others who helped him further develop this life-changing practice.

I hope this book honors his legacy as much as it's influenced me.

Several other names belong here, too:

W. Edwards Deming. One sentence of his lives in the back of every meeting I run: *If you can't describe what you're doing as a process, you don't know what you're doing.* Most failure I see — in agents, in brokerages, in real estate as a profession — comes from people who describe expectations but do not understand how to actually meet them. If you can't describe it, you can't teach it. If you can't teach it, you don't know it.

Theresa Barnabei. Terry Bass is named after her. Theresa and I meet most Fridays. She is the reason the thinking in this book is articulated as cleanly as it is. The book exists in this form because she has been willing, week after week, to sit across from me (on Zoom calls) and investigate wild rabbit holes. The insights we've both helped each other develop are poetic in their beauty. The most important thing about Theresa, despite all of her success in business and life, is that she encourages greatness from others.

Christene Marie. As a marketer and communicator, Christene is literally on a level nobody can compare with. I saw Christene present during a learning session as I began my transformation. I saw her present again at the Traffic & Conversions Summit in January 2024. Thanks to an introduction from Mark DeGrasse, I was able to start a great friendship I continually learn from. A lot of heart was put into this book thanks to her influence.

Other names worth mentioning: **Mark DeGrasse**, **Jeff J Hunter**, **Dustin Reichman** and the entire **7FL community**, **Steve Liddle**, **Gabriel Vangelatos**, **Jay Vics**, **Rich Scierka**, **Delroy Muschette**, **Atiba D'Souza**, **Janie Wood**, **Michelle Traweek**, **Johnell Woody**, **Tammy Hall**, **Megan VonDeylen**, and **Marilyn Bostick**.

What Wade does in this book — going from rock bottom to a life he can thrive in — took him about a year. That is also about how long it took me.

I am not Wade in a literal sense. I am a licensed real estate agent in name, but my real transformation happened as a marketer and consultant to real estate professionals. The mechanics of my business are different from Wade's. Our contexts will be different, but our arcs will be similar.

Mine ran from July of 2023 to the summer of 2024.

I had a year you wouldn't wish on anyone before that. We lost our boy in August of 2022. I lost my father in February of 2023. By June of 2023, my direct mail company was bankrupt and insolvent. I was not failing in the same context Wade was failing. My daughters were two and four at the time. But I knew, the way you know a thing you don't want to know, that I was a horrible husband and father. I didn't want that to continue.

I didn't have a Terry. Theresa and I had not started meeting yet — that came in late 2024, after the work was already underway. In 2023 and 2024 I had Goldratt's books. I re-read *The Goal* and felt the floor change. Then I bought every TOC book I could find — print, audio, the *Handbook*, anything that would hold the thinking until I could hold it myself. I drew clouds for my own life. I drew pipes for my own business. I asked myself *why* until the answer underneath each fear became visible. Most of what Wade does inside Terry's office, I did alone in mine.

Here is the part I hope you felt, despite the book never explicitly saying it:

The thinking becomes second nature only through practice, and you'll never practice well alone.

Practice is a never-ending series of refinements. One of my favorite ways to demonstrate this is to talk about Steph Curry, one of the best shooters in NBA history. As of this book's publishing, he's made 4,248 three-point shots in his career. He's the only player to ever accumulate over 4,000 three-pointers. He's also the only player to make over 3,000. However, what most people don't realize is that it's taken him an estimated one million shots over the course of his career. That practice will never be measured explicitly in a stat line.

Wade's year is the compressed version of that. Mine was a year too, but only because I read every day and tried something every week and was honest about what didn't work and adjusted. Some readers will internalize this faster. Most will take longer. There is no shortcut, and there are no slow learners in this work — only people who keep practicing and people who stopped.

If you finish this book and try to apply the framework once and it doesn't immediately work, ***that is the framework working***. The first attempt is not supposed to be perfection. The second is not supposed to be perfection. The third is not supposed to be perfection. You are not behind. You are in the thick of it, so stay in the thick of it.

The most important thing to remember, though, is you don't have to do this alone. Wade had Terry. Successful athletes like Steph Curry have their coaches and trainers. I have Theresa and dozens of other confidants who help me. Our transformations aren't exclusively due to the framework. The framework is the scaffold. We are social creatures who learn best when we are in a social setting. Wade learned to rely on people around him to improve. It was one of the hardest lessons I had to learn.

A workshop or a coaching program is not the most important thing I can offer, at least not yet. Right now, if this is your first time connecting with the thought processes in this book, I can be your Terry. If a person isn't available for you yet, then I'd be privileged to help. Also, I have created a host of resources at **homefordinner.co** that you may request access to.

When the appropriate time comes, Lesix Agency runs a program called the **90-Minute Marketing Department.** It is the operating system this book describes, built for real estate professionals to use without me having to be in the room 24/7. It is $47 a month, which is far less than most of the coaching and tools that are generally offered. To sign up for the 90MM, visit **90minute.ai**.

You aren't alone in this. It is okay to take your time. It is okay to accept the constraint as the constraint and live with it for a while before you change it. But do not face it alone.

Wade's first move — the one that began everything — wasn't a framework. It was a phone call to Terry, late at night, when he had run out of ways to avoid asking for help. He stopped pretending he didn't need it. The greatest place to start, after reading this book, is the same question he asked himself in his car that night:

Who can I call?

Statement on AI Use

I consider myself an early pioneer of the use of artificial intelligence, especially in real estate. I began using Claude in 2023 about four months after its public release. I teach the use of AI in an ethical manner in the real estate industry, consistent with industry standards and our code of ethics. I've developed a compliant and profitable way to build and use AI that is influenced by the way good management leads human employees. I use AI as a tool, albeit an entirely different tool from the way we understand hardware and software.

Therefore, I used Claude to write me the first draft of this book. Specifically, I built a plugin in Claude Code to draft the initial chapters according to specific research and information I provided. I used a Claude project to assist in ideation and organization of thoughts. Information provided included: book concepts, character notes, outputs from thinking processes and diagnostic tools. Most importantly, I provided extensive voice memo transcripts of me vocalizing my thoughts and ideas as training information.

The question I am sure I will get: why not hire a ghostwriter or work with a co-author? Truth is, I didn't want to. When it comes to writing, it's simply hard for me to start, but I will pour myself into revisions. And, in this case, I did. I hired a competent editor to review the first manuscript for voice, style, consistency, grammar, and all the things an editor might. That was after the initial draft and the first round of revisions. After his round of revisions, I continued with another round on my own that significantly changed portions of the book.

I understand and recognize people will refuse to read this book as a result. I also recognize and respect the negative reviews you might leave. I expect it, and to that I will say: You are not who this book is for or who will benefit the most.

Why?

The nature of Home for Dinner is to question conventional wisdom using a structured, systematic method. The same thinking process Wade went through in this book, I went through in my own life. This is a personal reflection of progress, and that's how human lives change. We share our thoughts with our language. Our language reflects the way our minds work, and by nature we are explorers.

Scanning the code below will take you to a video in which I go through an extensive review of the process I used. I encourage you to view it if you have questions. If you have more, you can schedule time with me directly at https://lesix.agency.

www.ingramcontent.com/pod-product-compliance
Lightning Source LLC
Chambersburg PA
CBHW031036160726
47991CB00005B/1895